Don't Call Me Madam

Don't Call Me Madam

The Life and Hard Times of a Gentleman Pimp

William Donaldson

MASON/CHARTER   NEW YORK 1977

First published in the U. S. by
Mason/Charter Publishers, Inc.

1 2 3 4 5 6 7 8 9 10

Library of Congress Cataloging in Publication Data

Donaldson, William.
    Don't call me Madam.

      1. Prostitution—England—London. 2. Donaldson, William.
3. Pimps—England—London—Biography.
I. Title.
HQ188.L8D66 1977   301.41′54′0924   77-1691
ISBN 0-88405-556-6

PREFACE

Since there is nothing more irritating than the private language of a colonial sub-culture, I include here for the American edition of this book a short glossary of difficult words. In compiling this, I have been guided by Eugene Ionesco's interesting contribution to the theory of meaning: "The French for London is Paris."

Business girl—Hooker.
Brothel—Cat house.
Cat house—House for cats.
Cambridge University—Harvard.
C.I.D., The Metropolitan—Detectives of the N.Y.P.D.
Clayton, Lucy—Eileen Ford.
Cricket, It's not—Un-American.
Darboigne, The Countess of—Xaviera Hollander.
Dumb insolence—Pleading the Fifth Amendment.
Edinburgh, the Duke of—Mrs. Jimmy Carter.
Evans, Dame Edith—Helen Hayes.
Godalming—Greenwich, Connecticut.
Gonk—John.
Grade, Lord Lew—Barnum and Bailey and Ringling Brothers and Sam Goldwyn and Coco the Clown.
Harrods—Bloomingdale's.
Hat, bowler—Brown derby.

Hird, Thora—Nancy Walker.

House spirit, Lack of—Not enough Rah! Rah! Rah!

Immorality—Sexual intercourse.

Intelligence, British—The C.I.A.

Lambton, Lord—Congressman Wayne Hayes.

Levy, Miss Norma—Miss Fanny Foxe.

London—New York.

Longford, Lord—The President of the Catholic Legion
            of Decency.

MacLauchlan, Ian "Mighty Mouse"—Joe Namath.

McLoud, Marshal Sam—Marshal Sam McLoud,

Manchester United—The New York Giants.

Mark, Sir Robert—The Commissioner of the N.Y.P.D.

Montgomery, Field Marshal—General George S. Patton, Jr.

Mug—John.

National security—National security.

Ponce—Pimp.

Popper, Sir Karl—Professor Hilary Putnam.

Punter—John.

Redgrave, Vanessa—Jane Fonda.

Shepherd's Market—Times Square.

Sloane Avenue—Park Avenue.

Snooker, In deep—Behind the eight ball.

Solicitor—Attorney.

Swapping—Swinging.

Tatler, The—Town and Country.

Wanker—One who suffers from Portnoy's complaint.

Wickstead, Bert "The old grey fox"—Eliot Ness.

White, Michael—Joe Papp.

Whitehouse, Mrs. Mary—The lady President of the Catholic
            Legion of Decency.

Wykehamist, An old—An alumnus of Groton.

World, The News of—The National Enquirer.

Don't Call Me Madam

Living in a brothel isn't everything it's cracked up to be. This struck me late yesterday evening as I tramped up and down the Fulham Road, banned from the premises until the last visiting fireman had been tipped into the night.

Perhaps I should have thought twice before accepting the job. That it was the first position of any sort offered to me in competitive circumstances since I graduated fifteen years ago no doubt over-impressed me. And the timing of the offer was most fortuitous. Determined to hang on in Ibiza, I was in a state of some uncertainty as to how best to do so. Should I promote a *Scrutiny* revival on the Island by opening a library with books miraculously hung on to since Cambridge? Or should I run an Indian restaurant in a bicycle shed behind the bull-ring?

It was fifty-fifty. Then providence in the shape of Miss Crampton the temporary secretary drops out of the sky with the not unforeseen news that she's now Emma Jane the call girl, with a place for me on the firm. The terms offered were the air fare back to London, full board and upkeep for the duration of the agreement, a small dress allowance and enough mad money to take my cronies out to lunch. This sounded like life with some of the problems removed, so I accepted. With assurances that I would follow shortly, I sent Emma Jane back to London to ply her trade against my arrival, and meanwhile decided that as I might be the only ponce with a pen it was of some importance that I keep a record of the various comings and goings. Since it is in the nature of things that those who

9

control the media are punters, ponces have never received a very good press.

Got back to London last Monday night and was surprised when the front door of Emma Jane's neat little flat in Sloane Avenue was opened by Black Dolores, of all people, disconcertingly topless and well spaced out on one of the euphoric drugs with which she arms herself against life's various tribulations. Small world. It seems that she took up the position of acting ponce the day after Emma Jane returned from Ibiza.

Not a coherent conversationalist at the best of times, Black Dolores, either from the shock of my arrival or the cumulative effect of the drugs, was on this occasion struck dumb. Unable to manage even her customary slurred "too much, Baby," she glared in my direction, moved unsteadily towards the bedroom, fell over suddenly like a parrot that's had a double brandy, hauled herself up, packed sourly and slunk away in the wounded manner of a stag bested in a territorial dispute, muttering something about "splitting to India to think things over." That made sense.

Elated by this immediate recognition of my status, I unpacked my Ibiza basket and hung up my suit in Emma Jane's wardrobe. This was stuffed to bursting with rather unsuitable Ossie Clark dresses (Emma Jane is arguably not tall enough to carry them off with much flair), but I took it as a reassuring indication that business is booming. Emma Jane seemed pleased to see me and showed no consternation at the abrupt withdrawal of Black Dolores. This was reassuring too, since I have learned over the years not to underestimate Black Dolores as a rival. Despite her customary condition, she has an awesome unity of purpose, which girls particularly seem to find most attractive. That she can dominate her environment so completely while apparently walking in her sleep is quite a conundrum in my opinion, but there it is.

I was then introduced to Big Elaine, who shares the flat and thus makes it by definition legally (or illegally) a brothel. I'm rather glad of this. There's little point in bragging that you live in a brothel if you don't.

Big Elaine, of whose existence Emma Jane warned me in Ibiza, turns out to be an extremely cheerful girl, though a trifle down the market, I'd have thought. Whatever else you might say about Emma Jane, you could never accuse her of not being a lady, bred as she is out of a retired sea-dog and one of those ferocious, three-piece ladies who all happened to be playing golf at The Royal Berkshire in September '39 and immediately returned to London to be bombed. This pedigree may turn out to be the secret of whatever success Emma Jane has as a whore. Some punters must want a substitute for their wives rather than an alternative.

Big Elaine said she was pleased to meet me, using, for reasons that struck me as mysterious at the time, a stage foreign accent. Subsequently, Emma Jane has explained that she always does this at first meeting, believing it to be alluring, but thereafter forgets. She has a rather pretty baby face, with nice eyes and a particularly sweet expression, but the rest of her is of tremendous proportions, and is not constituted, I would think, merely of puppy fat. She is compulsively friendly and constantly runs out of steam in mid-anecdote : a circumstance brought about by a combination of excess ballast and a need to communicate all the details of her life at once, after the manner of someone poignantly accustomed to other people walking away before she has been able to bring them up-to-date.

One shouldn't sneer, however, for this formula—bizarre thought it may seem—regularly brings in three hundred pounds a week. I have Emma Jane's word for this and since it is not customary for girls to exaggerate the achievements of other girls, I am inclined to believe her.

Emma Jane, who in contrast is as neat as a glove, doesn't give two stuffs for good manners and makes it embarrassingly obvious that she too finds it surprising that men should pay so much for such a noticeable absence of conventional feminine attractiveness. Her attitude, at least on the evidence so far, is one of frozen superiority, thawing from time to time into the relaxed exchanges one might expect between mistress of the manor and under-scullery maid. They're certainly an odd combination and I can't imagine how they came to cohabit. I suspect that Big Elaine, who is forceful as well as jolly, simply moved in one day with her intimidating collection of dresses, stuffed animals, china ornaments, wigs, gaudy knickers, romantic novels, bath essences and souvenirs from Toledo, and that Emma Jane, drugged by Black Dolores, didn't grasp the implications until it was too late. I don't suppose it's a problem of much significance. Since women are not accustomed to liking one another, they can hardly expect mutual regard to be a necessary condition of their sharing a home. Anyway, we shall see. If things become too disagreeable, I shall side with Big Elaine. In spite of her size, I take her to be the weaker party, and she did get here first. I don't suppose she was warned that I was part of the deal and I wouldn't want her to find my arrival a disruptive influence.

Meanwhile, the excitement of coming back to London had rather worn me out and I retired to watch television in bed. Emma Jane hadn't got up yet, so this arrangement suited her excellently. We watched a very funny piece called *Colditz*, which I mistook, having been out of things for a while, for an episode of *Monty Python*. Emma Jane pointed out my mistake and added that this series had rather offended Jerry.

"Surely you mean the British," I said.

Not a bit of it, insisted Emma Jane, it was definitely Jerry who felt himself to be libelled.

Since the series depicts the Germans as having all the virtues, not the least of which is a super-human patience in the face of unpardonable rudeness by the British, portrayed here as a bunch of defiant pip-squeaks, this is puzzling. On the evidence of this episode, the only case that could be made out against the Germans is that they were too thick to notice that the British were even thicker and that if let loose to continue the war, the Germans must have won. Another mystery is that the actors on our side are indistinguishable from the military in real life. Either they are mimes of hitherto unexampled brilliance, or they really are officers in the armed forces. Since we can safely disregard the possibility that they can act at all, never mind brilliantly, it follows that they really are soldiers. But if they are soldiers, what are they doing blundering round a television studio, keeping the half dozen or so of the Equity Membership who can do it a bit out of work? Wake up Plouviez and Snitcher, and meanwhile it's good to be back in London. This is not the sort of insoluble paradox that keeps you awake in Ibiza.

*　　*　　*

Apart from the unsettling business of being banished either to the Fulham Road or the King's Road whenever a punter calls, this is all very pleasant. Indeed, it has already crossed my mind that the anxiety free life-style may prove so seductive that I may never wish to change it. Even so, I can't see the household as presently composed staying together for long. I strive to create harmony, but both as pros and chaps Big Elaine and Emma Jane are too dissimilar. A profound difference I've noticed in the week I've been back is that Big Elaine *is* a pro, whereas Emma Jane is merely arsing about: working only when she needs the bread (as she now calls it under the malign influence of Black Dolores) or when there's nothing better on television. Big Elaine, on the other hand, derides the notion of a personal life and talks about "my business" with the reverential emphasis of a Jewish wholesaler. She points out several times a day that "I want money behind me" and she is particularly proud that she already has two thousand pounds locked away in a Building Society. (Tarts, I've discovered, have an emotional relationship with Building Societies, equalled only by their infatuation with actual bricks and mortar. I do not believe that their steady preference for this form of investment is motivated by financial considerations; it is rather that to tarts of Big Elaine's kidney, houses and Building Society accounts are symbols of that four-square respectability for which they paradoxically strive).

In fact, Big Elaine is a thoroughly nice girl from the provinces, whose habit of squealing like a tickled piglet at unexpected moments fails to disguise an essentially puritanical disposition. She's still a baby, so it's early yet to form conclusions, but I'm working on a theory that she thinks sex in all its manifestations a trifle rude and has therefore decided that charging for it is the least morally confusing thing to do. She certainly considers Emma Jane's proclivities, whether straight or otherwise, danger-ously unprofessional—like an addict having the run of John Bell and Croyden. That she has accepted me so painlessly into the set-up is explained, I think, by the fact that she finds me such an improvement on Black Dolores, who must have repre-sented everything that isn't nice. I'm male, after all, Caucasian, apparently straight and exceedingly polite. I suspect, however, that she thinks I'm too old to service the account, wherein she may well be right.

A cohesive element in their relationship may be that both were put to work by Chinese Vicky, who, while manageress of a shoe shop in Sloane Street must have sold fewer trendy boots than she sent customers the other way. Big Elaine tells me that she went in one day to make a purchase and came out with a date to spank Mr. X the illustrious film producer, who, between setting up grandiose epics and behaving sadistically towards his understrappers, likes to be ticked off by naughty girls. If Big Elaine visited me I'd call the cops myself, but Chinese Vicky clearly recognises three hundred pounds a week when she sees it. The explanation for this apparently disproportionate earning capacity seems to lie with Arabs, who prefer girls to be pleasantly soft in the head and built like combine harvesters.

Emma Jane's start in the business was likewise accomplished by Chinese Vicky, but the initiation proceedings were more protracted in her case. They met, it seems, a little over a year ago and at once embarked upon a small romance, in the course of which it was gradually borne in on Emma Jane that, as she puts it, "everyone on the gay scene does bits and pieces". For some time she rather felt herself to be the odd man out in this milieu, and it therefore came as something of a relief when Chinese Vicky at last invited her along on an assignment in the course of which money would change hands in return for favours granted. Emma Jane agreed immediately, because, as she says, "I didn't want to seem a fish".

Not wishing to seem a fish was a continuing state of mind and consequently her business throve. For several weeks she continued to work as a secretary in a theatrical agency, but eventually the absurdity of her double life became intolerable. Why, she asked herself, should she continue to slave away in a gloomy showbiz office, bored to stupefaction and insulted alike by leery executives and visiting mimes, for a miserable twenty-five pounds a week, when she could earn this precise sum in one hour each evening by dint of closing her eyes and giving her mind over to deep examination of her personal arrangements? Sanity eventually prevailed and the twenty-five pounds a week was allowed to go hang.

*   *   *

Big Elaine's habit of answering the phone in her alluring foreign accent has some strange consequences. Yesterday it rang and she said: "Ayloo—si si, theese eese Elaine, vot can ay do for you? Oh, hullo Mum, how are you?"

What can her mother think? I put this to Big Elaine fair and square and she said: "Oh, it's quite all right. She thinks I'm in catering."

That's too subtle for me.

Relations between her and Emma Jane have been steadily worsening ever since I moved in. Emma Jane—a sweetie in all other respects—is really vile to her. She hasn't confined her to her own quarters yet, but if she comes across one of Big Elaine's toys on supposedly communal territory, she picks it up—holding it gingerly away from her body between thumb and index finger as if it were infested—and drops it on the floor of Big Elaine's room with a disapproving "I think this must be yours".

She has taken particular exception to Big Elaine's record collection. This is a bit depressing—Noel Coward at Las Vegas, Oscar winning film themes, that sort of thing—and that it should be played as little as possible seems reasonable: that it should not be allowed on the same shelf in the sitting room as Emma Jane's trendier sounds, lest it infect them, is over-harsh, I think.

A less resilient girl than Big Elaine would be totally demoralised by now, and even she hardly dares to leave her room unless Emma Jane's out on business. She's a gregarious soul and on these occasions I naturally bear the brunt of her frustrated social energies. Unlike Emma Jane, she enjoys her work (this is because she finds sex funny; to Emma Jane sex is important and the professional need to dissemble brings her down) and the reports of her various encounters can be quite amusing. Indeed, were it not for these dispatches from the front I might suppose myself to be living in a laundry. (Emma Jane seems determined to turn my brothel into a home. This must be resisted. Since a brothel must be one of the few examples of a zoo in which the inmates have the laugh on the customers, it provides a continuously reassuring context for anyone who hides a driving need to see his superiors belittled behind a thin facade of affectionate self-disparagement.)

Not that Big Elaine's stories have any titillating value. By some mysterious and secret formula—only in the possession, I had hitherto supposed, of producers of blue movies—she manages to evacuate the most potentially stimulating scenarios of all erotic content, but her reports do have a certain sociological interest. The only time I can't be doing with her is very late at night when Emma Jane is out doing her thing and I've tucked myself into bed, either to read a book or watch television. Unfortunately, she takes all clear indications that I want to be alone— even those verging on the ill-mannered—as a direct challenge. Bouncing in like a great silly puppy demanding attention, she positions herself heavily between me and the means by which I'm attempting to divert myself. At least she doesn't lick my face or knock the milk over, though I suppose she might resort to such tactics if all else failed. So far, the need has not arisen.

For the first few minutes I ignore her totally, failing in every respect to acknowledge her presence in the room, but continuing to stare at the television screen with a terrible concentration as though Sir Lew Grade had at last cracked the secret of life's deepest mysteries and was now broadcasting his findings to the world. Or if I'm reading, I refuse to put the book down, but move my lips in an exaggerated fashion as my eyes follow the words, so that she can be in no doubt as to what my game is. Neither of these stratagems has the slightest staunching effect on her burbling flow, and I dare say we could keep it up all night, with me reading steadily on, while she rattles away about the inexplicable virility of Arabs or about the English Lord who thinks he can only get it on for schoolgirls but is in fact so dippy that the same old boiler can visit him three nights in a row in different disguises. "I didn't like the girl who came last night at *all*", he says to the outraged version of the same girl, "but you're sweet".

As often as not I'm only saved by the return of Emma Jane. One sour look from that quarter and Big Elaine retires to the side-lines with the half-defiant, half-chastened look of a footballer dismissed from the field of play.

* * *

The class of all call girls, I've now discovered, divides precisely into two distinct and incompatible sub-classes. Little mutual admiration exists between the two, and that Big Elaine belongs to one and Emma Jane to the other puts a severe strain upon our household. Whereas the sub-class of which Emma Jane is a member is bent clear across the board, Big Elaine and her like are out of kilter with what's acceptable to society only insofar as their profession is concerned; in all other respects they strive for social acceptance. Emma Jane and her friends had broken ranks and turned their backs on the traditional values long before they went on the game, but Big Elaine and her friends were, and are, implacably respectable. Emma Jane became a whore as soon as she discovered it to be the only way of financing a comfortable way of ilfe, independent of the more irksome of society's demands. Big Elaine became a whore so that she might make enough money to purchase such material trophies of success as precisely define membership in the middle class. By and large, Emma Jane and her friends are bisexual, accept a version of reality only perceived through the agency of hallucinatory drugs, have difficulty in getting out of bed in the morning and returning thereto at a civilised hour at night, are alert to fashionable trends and the latest acceptable sounds, spend their money sometime before they make it and are commendably together about what they're doing. On an official questionnaire they might well write "whore" against occupation. Nor is this an aggressive stance. They've been conditioned, indeed, to believe that their way of life represents a failure of some sort, but it's a failure with which they've come to terms. They also have a tendency to fall foul of the various law enforcement agencies, often a consequence of their willingness to fence any article that appears to have fallen off the back of a lorry. (Emma Jane has now admitted that the bulk of her expensive wardrobe was bought at the front door of a shoppie she'd never seen before).

By way of contrast, Big Elaine and her friends own small dogs of impeccable pedigree, rise with the lark, learn Spanish, keep books of account, shop at Harrods, like to dine out in Beauchamp Place, take winter holidays in Tenerife, embrace a moral code that might be thought repressive by the Guerrillas for Christ the King and keep in close touch with their mothers, who look and talk like Thora Hird. Much of their day is spent quacking away to each other on the telephone and in the course of these conversations their painstakingly acquired genteel accents slip disastrously in inverse ratio to their mounting indignation at some imagined slight to their respectability.

"I saw Assiz last night", Big Elaine will report. "He's not a very cultured person, if you know what I mean. As soon as you arrive he gives you a drink and makes you sit there with your tits hanging out, that sort of thing. At any rate, I said to him, I said, I said *here*, I said *look*, I said, don't speak to me like that, I'm accustomed to being treated like a perfect lady, so you can fuck off for a start. I didn't let him have nothing, if you know what I mean".

As it happens, I find greater favour with Big Elaine's gang than I do with Emma Jane's. They mistake me for an English gentleman and being keen to improve themselves, they listen to me attentively. Emma Jane's friends, on the other hand, tend in my company to suffer acutely from what I believe Dr. Rona M. Fields calls "truncated attention span". When I start to talk, their eyes glaze over and they either fall asleep or leave the room. Notwithstanding what they think of me, I find them charming, which is just as well, since they fall through the door at all hours of the day and night, whereas Big Elaine's associates have by and large been banned from the premises.

I have a particularly soft spot for Dawn Upstairs, who lives on the floor above. She used to be a successful dancer and must have been very lovely once, but she's thirty-three now and beginning to acquire the alarmed look of someone whose inheritance is running out. Why loss of privilege should be poignant when it happens to a woman, I don't quite understand. In our society an outstandingly attractive girl is the equivalent of a boy with an unearned income, but when a man loses his inheritance no feelings of pity are aroused, nor should they be. Dawn Upstairs tends to talk wistfully of happier times and she tries to draw me out on the subject of show business, mentioning names of friends she never sees and of whom, alas, I've never heard. Not that she ever stays in one place long enough to round a conversation off. High on anodynes of every sort, prescribed by some fashionable quack in return for favours granted, she floats away on a puff of fear that the last bus to happiness is about to leave. "Listen", she'll say, "I met this boy at Tramps last night. Like socially. I think he fancied me and that. I don't know. What do you think I ought to do?" But before you can tell her, she's up and away, with the distraught air of a gazelle that's seen visions. In a buoyant mood, however, her conversation is beguilingly original, scattered with pronouncements that derive their richly complex quality from abrupt disconnections and changes of pace. Last night, she suddenly said: "No, listen. I saw Shirley this morning. She's pregnant again so she's had to give up work. She's gone back to being a secretary, has Shirley". Later she said: "If I meet a man now and he fancies me and that, I say it's fifty quid and that's it. I've found it's the only way to have a social life".

She's sweet and lovely, and I've even managed to hit it off with her new ponce Steady Eddie, so called because he's kept himself in continuous employment for the last fifteen years. He's only thirty now, but was fortunate enough to be born with the right connections. His mother was on the game—and still is, as it happens—and his father was an Irishman who devoted twenty years to designing a new ballet shoe that would revolutionise the dance. Satisfied at last that he had come up with the answer, he took his work along to the authorities at Covent Garden. On being told that the existing design was more than adequate to all demands placed upon it, he flew off to Tahiti in disgust, where his nose has turned blue.

Steady Eddie looks like a Turkish wine waiter and I gather that ponces usually do. I take him to be an example to all other ponces and I watch his every move for hints and pointers. When I tried to emulate his moody walk, however, I ricked my back and had to have a lie down. He's only been with Dawn Upstairs for a few weeks, having moved on from Sophie the Madame in a transfer deal involving Basil the Black Actor. Dawn Upstairs is certain that he loves her. He has invited me to play chess with him, but I have declined and will continue to do so. To be dismissed in five moves by a bejewelled young cad in high heel boots would be too devastating.

*   *   *

I have won a small but significant victory. After tricky negotiations it has been agreed that, except in special circumstances, I will not henceforth be kicked out of the flat when punters call, so long as I promise to confine myself to the kitchen and there conduct myself like a mouse.

I have Big Elaine to thank for this improved state of affairs. Last night her motherly good nature compelled her to speak up forcibly on my behalf. Two gentlemen—a journalist and his photographer—were coming over to take pictures of her and Emma Jane (in poses thought to be too unconventional for the average model to undertake) to illustrate—obscurely, I thought —a forthcoming cookery book. They were by no means run of the mill punters, argued Big Elaine, but fellow professionals, engaged like themselves in the pursuit of an honest penny by the exploitation of the female form, and it would hardly bother them that I was on the premises, so long as I stayed discreetly out of whichever room was being used for the modelling session. It was absurd in these circumstances, she said, that I should have to ponce about in the cold.

Emma Jane looked aghast at this unexpected challenge to her authority and then wavered. Could I be trusted, she asked, to keep myself to myself? What on earth did she think I'd do? Hide until a moment of maximum indecency and then introduce myself surprisingly into the room yodelling like a Zulu? (I was reminded of a story Jonathan Miller once told me. While still practising medicine, he was consulted one day by a foxy little man, who on examination turned out to have severe burns on his backside. Dr. Miller asked how this had happened. The little man explained that he had recently discovered that his wife was having an affair with his best friend. Upset by this departure from the contract, he had made it his business to find out the time and whereabouts of the next piece of immorality. Having acquired the relevant information he had been able to conceal himself in an advantageous position at the appropriate locale. He had waited until a salient moment and had then leapt from the wardrobe, jack naked and with a lighted firework up his arse. "That taught them a lesson and no mistake", said the little man contentedly, and indeed it must have done).

I assured Emma Jane that no one, least of all the photographer and the journalist, would know I was in the flat, and she agreed at last to a trial run, I retired to the kitchen with a book (the memoirs of Nobby Stiles, as it happens) and the punters arrived shortly thereafter. I had just got to the incident involving the loss of Nobby's front teeth and the attempted strangulation of Dennis Law by an aggrieved Spaniard, when Big Elaine, coyly wrapped in a pink negligee which resembled a monstrous explosion of candy floss, came into the kitchen. Would I, she enquired to my surprise, care to watch the proceedings? They were, she implied winkingly, well worth watching. I'm as much as a key-hole Kate as the next girl, but my feeling was that any tableau featuring Big Elaine might give me the colly wobbles for life, on top of which, my powers of self-control having been questioned by Emma Jane, I didn't wish to see leery. I therefore declined the offer, without I hope, appearing either prudish or ungrateful. Half an hour later, Emma Jane herself put her head round the door to say that the modelling session had been completed and that I could now join the grown-ups.

I emerged rather diffidently, but was soon put at my ease by the two punters, who were absolutely charming. That I was shy and conscious of a need to justify my presence, whereas they were at their ease and chatty, I put down to the fact that they were not naughty boys, who had strayed embarrassingly from the straight and narrow, but fellow toilers in the rich vine-yards of erotica. So sure was I that this interpretation of their confident behaviour was correct that a gradual awareness of heavy under-currents in the atmosphere not normally identifiable when fellow professionals meet about their business rather dismayed me.

The first clear indication I received that there was something fishy going on came with the realisation that Big Elaine had gone off her head. One minute she was behaving normally—which is to say like a plump, jolly West Country girl, whose podgy fingers have dived once too often into the Cadbury's Milk Tray—and the next she had thrown herself into a mind-blowing impersonation of a sex-kitten on speed: pouting, posing, rolling her eyes and suddenly communicating in the absurd broken English of a bad actress playing the naughty au pair girl in a Ray Cooney farce. The photographer, who I had taken to be a man of the world like myself, far from gathering up his equipment at this point and walking into the night with suitable excuses, seemed to be captivated by this performance. Indeed he went so far as to arrange his face into the sleepy sneer that men over the age of thirty-five tend to mistake for an expression of moody sensuality, and it soon became apparent that whispered negotiations of a financial nature were taking place whereby he might become the recipient of more personal attentions than had hitherto been the case. This was bad enough—since a man doesn't like to be at the very eye of another man's arrangements—but worse was happening to my left, where, to my horror, the journalist was now paying court to Emma Jane. Squeezing his eyes menacingly, he had begun to speak, for reasons of his own, in an American accent.

Since I had been formally introduced as, of all things, Emma Jane's boy-friend (a classification that had made me wince) I was more than a little embarrassed by this turn of events. How a ponce would behave in this situation was clear enough. He would, presumably, openly encourage it, possibly going so far as to ask that the cheque be made out in his name. But a boy-friend? The circumstances seemed to demand that I now carry myself with a kind of languid, but not paralysed, cool: a role not easily assumed at my age, and particularly not after doing nothing more urbane for two years than cruising package tourists round the coast of Ibiza in a glass bottom boat.

Poise, after all, is everything in the drug culture and failure now in Emma Jane's eyes to measure up to the situation might entail the withdrawal of privileges so recently granted. I fell to wondering, therefore, whether the latest conventions required me to stay put—but loose—or to stroll nonchalantly back to the kitchen. Unfortunately, I was rather stoned by now, and when stoned the mind tends to examine each aspect of a situation in fanatical detail, before setting like concrete round some huge, and usually paranoid, irrelevancy. On this occasion, I was at first convinced that the new morality allowed me to stay where I was and even to participate in whatever lubricities were about to take place. To move would be clumsy, old-fashioned and self-conscious. That seemed clear. No clearer, however, than the precisely contradictory belief that immediately replaced it: the conviction that I ought to retire to the kitchen with all possible haste, since the present situation was by no means an example of the new morality in action, but on the contrary a scene being played out in accordance with much older conventions. The decision to leave the room, while undoubtedly correct, presented me immediately with a new problem: how to move without giving the impression that I was doing so. Fortunately, while I was trying to solve this, the negotiations both to left and right were brought simultaneously to a satisfactory conclusion.

How Big Elaine and Emma Jane stage managed *their* exits now provided a revealing illustration of their contrasting work methods. Big Elaine, still pouting and purring suggestively, was the first to move. Embodying every cliche of a Place Pigalle tart in a Forties Hollywood musical, save only that she failed to promise her companion "a nice time, cheri", she gathered up the photographer and led him by the hand to her bedroom. Emma Jane, however, immediately abandoned the relatively encouraging expression she had worn while the business details were being tidied up and now assumed the determined aspect of someone about to perform a necessary but unenthralling duty, such as cleaning the oven or taking the children out at half-term. Finally selecting the martyred, beds-don't-make-themselves look from the extensive repertoire of irritating feminine expressions, she walked briskly ahead of the journalist to her bedroom. Privileged though I'd undoubtedly been to see her on the job, so to speak, I couldn't help hoping, for all our sakes, that this wasn't her normal form. Perhaps my presence had been an inhibiting factor.

As was to be expected, Emma Jane's customer scarcely seemed to get his money's worth, and I only just had time to switch on *Come Dancing*—one of my favourites—before they were back in the sitting room. I was even more embarrassed now than I had been previously, but the punter was more at his ease than ever. This amazed me. On occasions when desperation and ineffectiveness have combined to send me to a professional, I've had the decency at least to slink away in the state of shock attendant on any abrupt drainage of self-esteem. The journalist, however, showed no such desire to creep away and hide. Perhaps he had to hang around for his friend (who, judging by the moans of simulated feminine ecstasy coming from Big Elaine's room, had made much the better investment), but even so the fool had no right, it seemed to me, to look quite so pleased with himself. Nor did he improve matters by switching off *Come Dancing*, without permission, putting on a Marvin Gaye record, sucking in his stomach and weaving round the room with the silly, self-regarding expression of a black croupier on his night off.

Now that the day's work was over, Emma Jane appeared to be in a rather more agreeable mood, though her observation, after one of the more outrageous groans of rapture emanating from the bedroom, that Big Elaine ought to join Equity, struck me as unprofessional. Even this clue that the conventions might be as formal as those governing the procedures of all in wrestling failed to ripple the surface of the journalist's composure. He opened his eyes a fraction, tried (and failed, incidentally) to click his fingers, and allowed himself a knowing, lazy smile. At last there was a shuddering, terminal groan from the bedroom, simultaneous with, and lasting the duration of, an astonishing sequence of events. Big Elaine contrived, I'm certain, to rocket out of the bedroom, run to the bathroom, return to the bedroom, emerged dressed, join us in the living room, flop into an arm-chair, lick a finger and count a wad of fivers, stuff them contentedly into her handbag, snap the handbag shut like a cashier closing the till in a supermarket, and enquire pleasantly whether anyone wanted a cup of tea because she jolly well needed one (her coquettish French accent quite forgotten and remaining, presumably, back in the bedroom along with the other appurtenances of her art) *before* the last echo of that thundering simulated climax had died away. That did the trick. The fantasies of even the most deluded middle-aged rocker could hardly be expected to survive such a cruel tidal wave of cold water. The journalist ceased abruptly to groove along with Marvin, the photographer emerged from Big Elaine's room looking thoroughly crumpled, they exchanged a few sheepish words, announced that it was time to go home, said good-bye and left.

In bed later, I offered some tentative criticisms of what I had taken to be a somewhat inadequate performance by the home team. I realised only too well, I said, that whores without exception felt nothing but a perfect contempt for their clients, but was it not counter-productive to evince it so clearly? Should it not remain a back-stage secret, so to speak? To my great surprise, far from accepting these mild and, I'd have thought, sensible observations in good part, Emma Jane became cross.

What on earth, she asked, did I know about it? Damn all, she said, answering her own question, and she'd thank me to belt up. I was stupefied. All men cherish private delusions.

My fancy is a steady belief that no vice operation on earth could be so well run that I couldn't run it better. This being so, naturally I became cross too. I pointed out that this was by no means the first time that I had found myself on this side of the footlights. Had I not served an apprenticeship with the Countess of Darboigne after she had come to live with me and Mrs Mouse, bringing with her Motor Show Polly and Mad Anna? And had I not studied her work methods so diligently that on two or three occasions at least I had been trusted to take bookings in her absence? (I made errors of a minor nature, admittedly, as any apprentice will. Once I told a nicely spoken gentleman, who had telephoned for Motor Show Polly, that she was entertaining some Arabs at the moment, but that Mad Anna— an even nicer girl—could be booked at the same price, only to discover that it was Motor Show Polly's father to whom I was speaking. And some of the Countess's methods struck me as being rather too thick-ear for emulation. One night Mad Anna didn't declare all the proceeds of an assignation and an ugly confrontation took place on the top landing. The Countess is knee high to a bee and beside Mad Anna even Big Elaine would look petite, but the Countess stood on tip-toe and let go with a right cross that lifted Mad Anna head over heels down one flight of stairs, *round a corner* and down a second flight, till she came to rest, hurt and startled, in the hoover cupboard in the hall. This, I decided, was an effectiveness I could never hope to equal). This rehearsal of my qualifications cut as much ice as a feather. Emma Jane merely snorted. I didn't know what I was talking about, she said, and she'd thank me not to poke my nose into her business in future.

This has left me feeling very despondent. If I'm not to be allowed to offer mild criticisms, let alone play any active part in the management of the firm's affairs, life is going to be very boring. This has led me to brood about a ponce's precise function. I have always supposed that the term "ponce" has a sense that is not exhausted by the substitution of the term "stud". A ponce is, after all, usually, though not tautologically, a man, and for this reason alone might be expected to be in a good position (customers being male on the whole) to offer a piece of advice here, a suggestion there, even perhaps to drum up a little discreet business. But if he's on the team merely for his virility quotient, then I'll get my cards (not that I have any) in no time at all. I clearly didn't give this matter enough thought before coming back to London and knocking on Emma Jane's front door. It never occurred to me that in the two years I was away, she might have acquired a degree of mental independence. When she was my secretary, I exercised, though I say it myself as shouldn't, power of attorney over her opinions, but now she seems to be verging on having a will of her own. This is very unsettling, and the question is: how can I hope to control her brain while living in her flat, eating her food, accepting her pocket money and allowing her to refurbish my wardrobe? (There is some rivalry among whores in the matter of their ponce's wardrobes. This makes sense. A scruffily turned out ponce reflects adversely on the earning capacity of his benefactor and she consequently suffers a loss of prestige. At first I found Emma Jane's dismay at my appearance comical and my reaction was to club her into silence with a line or two of Auden.

"Only tuneless birds/inarticulate warriors/need bright plumage", I said.

"Bull shit", she said. Very bad luck Magdalene, as Bamber would say, just behind on the buzzer there. Among my other troubles, culture, I can see, is going to be on the Index). I can get away with all this only by maintaining a sexual performance laughably beyond my capabilities. My days are numbered, I feel, and I must turn my attention to alternative ways of earning my living. Moral scruples must give way to expediency and I must re-establish diplomatic relations with the world.

* * *

Have continued to brood for the last few days about Emma Jane's sudden acquisition of officer-like qualities. By modifying my behaviour uncomfortably I've managed to avoid any unfortunate disputes, but her new authority is disconcerting. She isn't consistently tyrannical, but her easy assumption of moral superiority, as she patrols her territory, on the lookout for imperfections or traces of slovenly behaviour, is most exacting. The peculiar ability to make you feel you've committed a misdemeanour even when you haven't, backed up by power of deduction bearing a greater resemblance to the paranatural than to any known laws of valid inference, is given, of course, unilaterally to women (this being so, it is hardly surprising that the dottier elements in women's lib have been able to make *men* feel guilty, even though it is self-evidently men themselves who society has compelled to act out the more inhibiting role; the exhortation "be a man!" is a stage direction, not a suggestion that one gets oneself the appropriate supply of male hormones), but that little Emma Jane, who two years ago wouldn't have said boo to a goose, should have acquired such towering moral ascendency amazes me. It's a confusion of ethical and territorial rights, of course. Take her outside and she'd be as unsure of her position as a kitten in a bull-ring. This knowledge, however, is little comfort to me and Big Elaine. While we're on her territory she's confident enough to make us mind our p's and q's. The pity is, it's all so unnecessary. A tart's setup is an economy of abundance if ever I saw one and repressive measures ought to be superfluous.

Big Elaine and I have discussed the matter at one of the clandestine production meetings we hold first thing in the morning before Emma Jane has risen, and we have decided that she should have a soubriquet that adequately reflects her newly acquired gravitas. Having considered the various possibilities, it seems to us that only Chief of Detectives Robert T. Ironside, of the excellent television series, evinces day in and day out, in all situations and all weather, the steady sagacity and omipotence that we recognise and defer to in Emma Jane. We propose henceforth to call her "Chief."

*   *   *

Came home today from a little walkabout to find the Chief blubbing. Rather shocked by this definitively un-Chief-like collapse, I asked her what was the matter. She explained, between sobs, that a friend's flat was burglarised this afternoon, and it seems that suspicion has fallen upon my friend S. Z. Corbett.

27

The evidence, which is only circumstantial, is as follows. During the time that S. Z. Corbett was the Chief's house-guest, her friend Lucy went away on holiday, leaving the key to her flat in the Chief's possession so that she might go in to feed the cat. This key disappeared at the same time as S. Z. Corbett was removed from the Chief's flat by Black Dolores, but no causal connection was established or even suspected. Apparently S. Z. Corbett was the only person apart from the Chief who knew to whose flat it was the key, and this is enough to convince her that he is the culprit.

Worse things happen at sea, I said, but she refused to be comforted. I wouldn't suppose that she's against burglary in principle, so I imagine the extent of her upset is explained by the personal element involved. I'm very sorry about this. Women tend to be rather inflexible in these matters and I expect S. Z. Corbett will be blackballed for life. This would be a shame. He's a bit of a rascal, but I'm very fond of him; certainly fonder than I am of the Chief's friend: a thin-legged and snooty lady, who on such occasions as I've met her has looked me up and down as though I'm something her cat's rejected. She's no better than she should be, in my opinion, and such baubles as she may have lost would, I suspect, have been immorally come by.

The Chief's reaction to her new rank has been interesting. At first she rather took to it, interpreting it correctly as a mark of our respect. Gradually, however, she has come to believe that we are taking the rise and she has actually forbidden us to so address her in the future. It is a measure of her total domination over us that we ceased to do so instantly, at least to her face. Behind her back we continue to refer to her as the Chief, there being the added thrill that we know a terrible retribution will be visited upon us if we're caught. The whole incident has been a perfect demonstration of Laing's Law: Rule A "don't;" Rule A1: "Rule A doesn't exist;" Rule A2: "do not discuss the existence or non-existence of Rules A, A1 or A2". Nice one Ronnie, and precisely how the loving head of any household maintains discipline and a tight ship. Emma Jane *is* the Chief, but the fact must be tacitly assumed, never articulated. Boys will be boys, so the occasional breaking of Rule A is inevitable; but failure to observe Rules A1 and A2 is inexcusable.

* * *

Since coming back to London, I have seldom ventured further away from command module than *The Goat in Boots* in one direction and Daft Des, the local newsagent, in the other. But yesterday, in accordance with my resolution to live more daringly, I sallied forth with every intention of walking all the way down the King's Road. I was proceeding cautiously toward World's End, thinking to myself that this wasn't so bad, but ready to duck and dive at the first indication of trouble (bearing in mind the undesirable social elements to be found in this neck of the woods—wallpaper hangers, actors, hairdressers, models, creators of ladies underwear, rock and roll singers, choreographers, jugglers etc.) when I bumped into two of the nicest people you could hope to meet in a long day's march : 'arding the King's Road totter, looking angelic in white velvet, accompanied by the equally lovely Sarah. They were struggling to squeeze an expensive looking desk through the door of an antique shop, so in case they were trying to nick it, I went to their assistance. When I told them of my whereabouts and occupation, 'arding, once he was satisfied I was on the level, looked at me with absolute respect for the first time in all the years I've known him, and Sarah said :

"A ponce? How super! Just like my husband".

'arding rounded on her with a snarl of contempt.

"Don't be so fucking *stoopid* Sarah! Willie's a *real* ponce, not a *wanking* ponce like your fucking 'usband. 'Oo' you poncing off then?"

"My ex-secretary".

" 'Ere, straight up? Not the tasty one what sat in reception? I really reckoned 'er". 'arding was silent in contemplation for a moment and then summed up his thinking on the matter. "I could of given 'er one as it 'appens".

"Alas no", I said, "not her, the other one".

I was so delighted to see them that I asked them to dinner the same evening. This may have been going beyond my brief, but the occasion went without a hitch. The food and wine were excellent and the conversation, thanks to 'arding's disinclination to talk about anything other than the idiosyncracies of Emma Jane's clients, most stimulating. Rather to my surprise, Emma Jane obliged with a wealth of detail that might have offended against good taste on a more formal occasion. Clearly it is only with me that she is reluctant to talk about her business. This encourages me, since it implies that there is no fundamental block, but merely a small impediment vis-a-vis myself, which can easily be removed. Eventually 'arding, his eyes out like chapel hat pegs, said :

"Fuck me, 'ow I'd like to live in a brothel. It's me fucking fantasy. Sarah, why don't you become a brass?"

"Would you like me to?"

"*Course* I'd fucking like you to. There's nothing I'd like more as it 'appens. Not that you could; you're too fucking *stoopid*".

It seemed wrong that someone who had not so long ago been one of London's top models should be dismissed so summarily, and I intervened accordingly :

"In my opinion Sarah would make an absolutely first-class brass".

"Thank you. Do you really think so?"

"Certainly".

'Bollocks", said 'arding.

"Don't say bollocks like that. Willie knows more about it than you do".

"As it 'appens", said 'arding, "as it *'appens*, I know a fair bit about it. In fact it may interest you to know that — wanted to go on the game, but only if I manage 'er".

"Why didn't you?"

"She went and got a part in some fucking musical, didn't she? Playing the Virgin Mary. No, straight up. Still, we 'ad some great scenes. 'Ere, you know 'ow sex is never as good as a wank? I mean it's okay, but wanking's better, right? Well, if you take Mescalin, fucking's as good. Straight. I used to go round to 'er pad, and she and 'er girl friend from the Eve Club and me used to take Mescalin and then 'ave a scene. No, honest, after taking Mescalin, *fucking's* as good as *wanking*".

I was wondering whether 'arding, who I've always taken to be the Walter Pater in these matters, might not have a point here—that indeed all sex aspires to the condition of masturbation —when Big Elaine, who had been out all evening on business, phoned to say that she was behind with her bookings and that a punter might turn up at the flat before her return. Would we be so good as to entertain him until her arrival? He was, she said, a most cultured person and a bank manager to boot. This prospect was much too exciting for 'arding, and he insisted that we set the poor fellow up like the last pin in a bowling alley. After some discussion (in which, revealingly enough, Emma Jane played an active role, though were such a jape to be perpertrated on one of *her* clients, her wrath would bring the building down), it was decided that Sarah should dress up as a naughty maid and that 'arding and I would pretend to be punters also waiting for Big Elaine. I agreed to this on condition that the game didn't get out of hand, exposing me as first cab off the rank on her return.

Emma Jane took Sarah into the bedroom for a wardrobe fitting and I fell to wondering whether fate might not have delivered into my hands that silly old goat, Mr. Bottle of the hard heart and wall-eye (a disturbing imperfection in a bank manager, since good manners required one to direct one's gaze off-centre rather than directly at his handicap, thus running the risk of seeming furtive, which is the very last impression one is trying to give when explaining some minor confusion in the management of one's affairs). When Sarah came back into the living room, she was wearing black stockings, a suspender belt and a little white handkerchief serving as an apron. She looked jolly good, and it seemed most unlikely that the bank manager, unless he was some sort of deviant, would care to wait for Big Elaine; which was precisely the thought that seemed to cross 'arding's mind at this moment.

" 'Ere Sarah", he said, "you don't look to bad, as it 'appens. I could almost fancy you meself. Play your cards right and you could make yourself a lazy two five".

That Sarah should earn herself a little mad money by pulling the bank manager seemed like a good idea, so the scenario was modified accordingly. It was decided that, as soon as there was a ring on the door bell, 'arding should conceal himself under the bed in Big Elaine's room, whither Sarah would endeavour to tempt the bank manager before the arrival of Big Elaine. That his fantasy was so close to realisation had put 'arding into a terrific state of excitement, but Sarah became a little apprehensive now, as well she might. No-one knew better than she that 'arding would give her a backhander if she failed in her assignment and another, in all likelihood, if she didn't.

The bank manager duly arrived and I was momentarily disappointed that he was not Mr. Bottle, but an enormous man, sporting a Battle of Britain moustache and an R.N.V.R. tie : an odd mingling of traditions. If Sarah failed to pull the trick, it seemed the building might be at risk. He and Big Elaine would couple with the impact of two Sumo wrestlers colliding in mid-ring, and unless the floor had been reinforced against such a contingency, it seemed likely that Big Elaine, the bank manager, 'arding and the bed would be dropping in on the family below for an impromptu late night drink.

Not that there seemed much danger of our scheme going wrong. That flesh and blood (even the thin, watery variety flowing sluggishly through a banker's veins) could resist Sarah looking as she did was not to be conceived. And she played her role to perfection, blending diffidence and flirtatiousness in ravishing proportions. Such was the effect on me of this subtle and lovely performance that it was quite some time before I noticed that it was making no impact upon the bank manager whatsoever. He was courteous and correct, as I suppose bank managers are trained to be, but quite unmoved. In the face of such impassiveness, Sarah became desperate and, mindful no doubt of the expectations of her consort under the bed, she went over the top. Perching herself provocatively on the bank manager's massive knee, she issued an unambiguous invitation.

"Thank you dear", said the bank manager politely, "but I think I'd prefer to wait for the other lass".

Scarcely credible! Among the class of true propositions, one alone, I'd have thought, could be advanced in any part of the world without fear of rational contradiction or a challenge to come out on the cobbles : namely that no man, of any political, religious or cultural persuasion, of any age or in any physical condition, drunk or sober, in or out of his right mind, trying to win a bet or on his honour to guard his country's secrets, would, in these or any other circumstances real or imaginary, in the past, present or future, prefer Big Elaine to Sarah. Which goes to show how much I know about the business. Emma Jane is quite right. I'm an amateur and it would behove me to keep my advice to a minimum. There was nothing we could do but wait for the return of Big Elaine and speculate to ourselves about who was the worse off : we who were stuck making desultory small talk with this eccentric giant, or 'arding, his fantasy in ruins, compelled to sit it out under the bed until the banker had had his pleasure of Big Elaine. Which might take all night.

There was a happier ending than we deserved. Big Elaine's return was not long delayed and once she had got the bank manager into the bedroom the strain was off the three of us, if not off 'arding. My only worry now was how Big Elaine would react to the inevitable discovery that an intimate moment in her affairs had been shared by a stranger under the bed. A degree of indignation seemed permissable, but as it turned out I need have had no fears. After the bank manager had at last departed, we congregated in the sitting room for a rather sheepish post-mortem and Big Elaine immediately proved her good nature to be inextinguishable. Far from being cross, she seemed to find the matter as diverting in retrospect as we had in anticipation and she even went so far as to thank us for looking after a client so well. What a splendid girl she is.

As for 'arding, he'd had the time of his life; far better, he said, than if Sarah had been able to upstage Big Elaine. The reason for this, it transpired, was that the bank manager's scene had turned out to be rather more imaginative than his appearance and personality would have suggested. 'arding speaks as he finds, and unmindful of whether Big Elaine would wish such trade secrets to be broadcast, he reported lip-smackingly on the little production to which he'd just been secretly privy.

The bank manager's pleasure, apparently, was to pretend to be a chorus girl rather too easily led. Dressed in Big Elaine's underwear (this explained his otherwise irrational preference for her: no other girl's would fit him) he sat meekly with bowed head, Battle of Britain moustache drooping with shame, while Big Elaine, playing another chorus girl (dance captain, perhaps) gave him a terrific wigging for going out with stage door Johnnies. 'arding's only regret was that he'd failed to discover over which branch of which bank the good fellow presided. No doubt he felt that the nearest he'd ever get to an unsecured facility had come and gone. Big Elaine claimed that she had the necessary information, but wisely refused to divulge it.

A very pleasant evening and I'm confident we'll be seeing a lot more of 'arding, if rather less of Sarah. A lady who has spent the best part of an hour running around in nothing more sub-stantial than a handkerchief, and all to no avail, needs rather more reassurance than 'arding is of a composition to provide. She went away looking rather sad.

* * *

Max Beerbohm's remark that "women are a sex on their own, so to speak", has always seemed to me to be there or thereabouts. Last night there wasn't anything much on television, so I offered for discussion the not outrageously controversial (as I saw it) proposition that if two people are sharing a home it is desirable that they should get to know each other : that they should be as well acquainted, for instance, as a man is with another man with whom he lunches twice a year. To this end, I said, it is desirable that the couple who are living together should, from time to time, communicate their true thoughts. No sooner said than Emma Jane burst into tears, and when I asked her what might be the matter, she screamed : "Don't touch me! don't touch me! You're despicable, leave me alone!" So I did. Whereupon, in a sharp one-two, she caught me up the kilt and poured a bottle of milk over my head. In the ensuing fracas, I was fortunate enough to get her early on in a combined head scissors and Boston crab, and had I not been looking lively in this respect the damage (to myself) might have been serious. As it was she sobbed for the next three hours, and though her reasons will remain obscure to me forever, I've learned enough from the incident to keep my trap shut in future. What, after all, would a man know about civilised behaviour within a relationship?

* * *

Basil the Black Actor came round this evening. I don't think he's too happy with the deal he's got with Sophie the Madame. The grub's good, he says, but he feels himself to be intellectually deprived. Sophie doesn't seem able to grasp that he's a serious artiste.

"You know how it is, old chap", he said, "it's all knickers

in the bathroom and where were you last night? Bay Jove, how a man panes for some serious conversation".

He's by Sporting Life out of Cardew 'The Cad' Robinson and declaims his lines with the ringing enunciation of a bit player at Stratford determined to make his mark in *Henry IV Part I*. He's frightfully grand. He has a pencil moustache and has recently taken to wearing a bowler hat. He can be extremely entertaining for about three quarters of an hour, which is rather better than par for the course. The obsessional nature of a mime's relationship with himself is usually only funny for about half this time. He has written the book, music and lyrics of a musical, and is now wondering whether there exists an entrepreneur of sufficient taste to co-present it with himself. He asked my advice on this point, and I suggested my old friend Diamond Pat Clancy, with whom I once ran a theatrical agency. Diamond Pat has now retired from show business and is thought to be back in Australia, selling plastic bogs to the Aborigines, the very thing he was doing before I persuaded him to join me in the laughter and heartbreak of the live theatre. Basil the Black Actor looked beady and said that a condition of any co-production deal was that he should play the lead, supported by Vanessa Redgrave. In that case, I said, Diamond Pat might not wish to become involved, since he had a low opinion of Miss Redgrave's talent.

Basil the Black Actor then asked me whether I had any plans to improve my own circumstances and when I admitted that I had none, he frowned disapprovingly and said :

"You gotta keep busy, man. Then if you fuck up you can say 'Well, at least I was busy'. But if you do nothing and you fuck up, man, I mean that's *heavy*".

In the middle of all this, S. Z. Corbett smuggled his way through the door, disguised as Emma Jane's friend Black Danielle. Emma Jane herself went to answer the ring and, looking through the spy-hole, mistook him for her girl-friend. He was through the door and in the living room with his feet up before she could rectify her mistake. I must say, if he did burglarise her friend's flat, he's got a lot of front. I asked him how life was treating him and he said not too well. It seems he's moved in with some girl who's proving most unreasonable. She's reluctant to go to work to keep him in the style to which he feels his remarkable good looks and sweet nature entitle him. I asked him whether he'd tried slapping her round the face. Certainly, he said, but she still refused to go to work. Then he said: "It's her flat and I threw her out one time already". I thought this was rather good, so I wrote it down on the back of a cigarette packet. This made every one very nervous for some reason, and the conversation didn't flow for a while. It picked up, however, when Basil the Black Actor unexpectedly announced in his ringing Edith Evans voice: "I'm as randy as an Arab as it happens and could do with some pussy. S. Z., my dear fellow, do you have any pussy at your beck and call?" S. Z. Corbett, sensing a mug, perked up and asked Basil the Black Actor whether he had any money on him. This was a ground floor mistake of the sort that starts world wars, since the very first lesson is 'never promote a promoter'. Immediately, Basil the Black Actor's eyes turned yellow with rage, his R.A.D.A. diction went for six and he leapt screaming to his feet. He put the tip of his nose within two inches of S. Z. Corbett's and screeched: "You said a silly thing then, man. *Nobody* asks me whether I've got money, *nobody*. You understand that, man? I say *shit* to money. Of course I got money, man. What you take me for? Anyone who ask me whether I got money get a bottle in his face!" S. Z. Corbett didn't seem too worried (and nor indeed did Emma Jane, which wasn't so surprising since women have an insatiable taste for this sort of altercation, thus giving the lie to the amazing theory that there would be less international bloodshed were women to be placed in charge of foreign affairs), but I became alarmed and tried to calm Basil the Black Actor down.

"Of *course* you've got money", I said, "piles of it, in fact. Good Heavens, everyone knows *that*".

"Certainly I've got money", he said "I never go out without it. I always have my fare home, in case there's violence". Then he asked whether he might have a word with me in private.

I took him into the bedroom and at first it seemed that he was going to work himself up into another rage. " How dare that fellow ask whether I have money! Who is he? What are his credentials?"

I explained that he was an old friend of mine. "I see. Bay the way, old chap, I seem to have left myself a little short. Could you possibly lend me fave pounds?"

I obliged, reluctantly, with my lunching out allowance for the next two days. Quite appeased now, Basil the Black Actor gathered up S. Z. Corbett and the two of them went off happily into the night in search of pussy. Basil the Black Actor left his bowler hat behind, and I may take to wearing it round the house. Inside there's a label which says "Property of A.T.V." But then, what isn't?

*　　*　　*

Within a pairing situation, call girls are, to my chagrin, just like other girls, but more so. (More so, I suppose to compensate for their occupation). Emma Jane, for instance, has a concept of relationships that might be termed Platonic. That is to say, she subscribes to the belief that there is an objective, ideal Relationship, somewhere up in the sky, to which all earthly forms should endeavour to approximate. Individuals should re-shape themselves, however painfully, so that their relationship bears an adequate resemblance to the Idea in heaven; they should not try to adapt the earthly copy to suit their personalities. It's a coherent notion, though mistaken in my belief, and now I've twigged it, things may go more easily. I shall spend less time gossiping with Big Elaine about business (which fascinates me, but which even I can see has nothing to do with a Relationship) and more time practising togetherness with Emma Jane. As a start we've acquired an adorable Siamese pussycat. We've called him Bernard and we can now communicate in the language suitable to a relationship. Last night, for instance, we watched different films on television, I in the living room, Emma Jane in the bedroom. Bernard chose to watch the same one as her. When it was over, she came back into the living room.

"Who did Bernard sit with then?"

"You", I admitted.

"Who does he love the best then, his Mummy or his Daddy?"

"His Daddy".

"Why did he stay with his Mummy then?"

"To make his Daddy jealous".

As luck would have it, this sort of thing comes pretty naturally to me.

*   *   *

In spite of my good intentions, I had a bit of a barney tonight with Emma Jane over my refusal to attend a party given by my friend Twigg the well-known Playwright, whom I'm never much cared for, I must say, and particularly not on a Saturday night. Would Dennis Weaver be there? I asked. What on earth, said Emma Jane, had that got to do with it? Everything, I said, because if he hadn't been invited I'd rather stay at home and watch *McLoud*. Emma Jane found this attitude absurd, not to say vexatious, but it seems to me to be perfectly sensible. Vast sums of money are spent and a great deal of thought and talent of a rare quality are brought to bear on the production of this particular piece of entertainment. Why should my friend Twigg the well-known Playwright suppose that by convening a few bores, passing round a bottle of Spanish Claret and generally creating a mood of blood-chilling *aprés-ski* cheerfulness, he might produce a valid counter-attraction? It simply doesn't make sense, but Emma Jane considers this point of view to be unhealthy, and quite possibly immoral. And others share it. If I had a pound for every occasion that someone has told me that watching television is a waste of time, I'd be a rich man. And if it *is* a waste of time, how are we to describe the absolutely balls-aching tedium of being trapped in a corner of a strange room by a copywriter one has never previously met or by a pub actor with a grudge? So Emma Jane went on her own, and came back after an hour looking virtuous. "Did you enjoy yourself?" I asked. "Not really", she said, "but one ought to go out". I don't understand this at all.

*   *   *

Emma Jane arrived home last night in a terrible state, but quite unable to tell me what was amiss until I had popped her into bed with a mug of hot chocolate. (Ponces are the equivalent of corner men, I've discovered. Their function is to comfort, patch up and offer philosophical advice between rounds so that the main contenders can stumble forward, in some sort of shape, to

38

continue the battle.) She'd had a date with an M.P. (Conservative) at the Mayfair Hotel and there had been a vulgar altercation over money. She and Black Danielle had put on a small cabaret for the M.P. and a jaded friend. After the monkey business, they'd been offered twenty pounds each. They'd pointed out that while pleasure was to be derived from what they'd just done—when done in private—it was quite another story when watched by two coarse old sods in their socks, and was customarily rewarded to the tune of thirty pounds apiece. This was too steep, the M.P. had insisted, whereupon Black Danielle had lost her rag and threatened him with every kind of retribution, from blowing the whistle on him to the Chief Whip to unmanning him on the spot. The M.P. had become apprehensive (as well he might, bearing in mind that Black Danielle looks like Brenda Arnau's bodyguard and is reputed to have won the catching the javelin contest five years running in her native Sierra Leone) and eventually they'd been able to extract a promise that the full amount would be forwarded by mail the following day. I ticked Emma Jane off. How, I asked, could she take the word of a common politician? And as for reporting him to the Chief Whip, how could she be sure he wasn't the Chief Whip?

*　　*　　*

The contempt in which call girls hold their gonks is comprehensive and would be bewildering to the gonks themselves were they not too self-satisfied to see the truth. Many of them are our leaders, after all, men who are accustomed to being treated with the respect that they feel their achievements deserve. All are successful, some even conventionally attractive. But to business girls they are merely gonks and their company is so appalling that they are charged ruthlessly by the minute. One hour, twenty-five pounds; dinner and hey-diddle-diddle, forty pounds; all evening, fifty pounds, all night, one hundred pounds. Some gonks, pointing out that dinner in the best restaurants costs money, argue that they should pay less because of the added hospitality. Business girls are insultingly scornful of this point of view. "Who the hell needs dinner with a gonk?" they reason.

Last week Emma Jane received an invitation (embarrassingly enough through a connection of mine in the film world) that most straight girls would have leapt at. It was to go to Rome first class as a surprise present for the director of a film being shot there. Emma Jane said that she would want at least three hundred pounds plus bits and pieces. I expostulated with her on the grounds that it had not been unknown for people to *pay* to visit Rome and that the gonk involved was young and not celebrated for his unattractiveness to women. Emma Jane snorted with derisive laughter. A gonk was a gonk, she said, and there was an end to the matter. I put the job around, but no-one would take it at the price offered £100) and I had to report back to my incredulous friend that I had failed completely.

It's a sad fact that the moment a man is prepared to pay cash he forfeits all dignity so far as the business girl is concerned. Punters, accustomed as they are to receiving the respect of all right-thinking people, don't seem able to grasp that to call girls they are *definitively* absurd. I can understand gonks whose somewhat abnormal desires are not to be easily satisfied by wives and girlfriends, or gonks who are masochists, and therefore want a humiliating relationship. But the majority seem to be straight and go to heart-breaking lengths to give the business girls a good time. Seemingly unaware that behind her plastic smile his paid companion is hiding murderous thoughts and ticking off the seconds until she can get home to some moody little bugger in high heel boots (who is putting a value on his time as ruthlessly as his benefactor is on hers) our eminent gonk pops another bottle of champagne, drapes his body langourously across the bed and embarks upon an inventory of his achievements. Sexual frustration is indeed a terrifying leveller.

Had lunch today with my friend Scott and we discussed this and related matters. He finds my contempt for gonks a trifle overdone, and suggests that it has been aggravated by the long hours I've had to spend shut up in the kitchen. While he admits that a man is not likely to be at his most attractive when paying for sex, it does not follow that such a man will be contemptible in any other context. He takes the view—shared, I must admit, by everyone with whom I've discussed the matter—that the treatment handed out recently to Lords Lambton and Jellicoe verged on the scandalous. I'm not sure. I can't help feeling that a man who is consistently deluded (if only in one respect), who consistently puts himself in a humiliating situation, without seeming to realise that he is doing so, must be a lightweight. My friend Scott doesn't agree with this view. All of us, he says, are liable from time to time to become slightly unbalanced by sexual desire. Certainly, I say, and those of us who are unbalanced several times a week are unsuitable for high office. Rubbish, says Scott. There is no reason to suppose that sexual looseness affects one's ability to function adequately in other areas. What, I ask, if one's desires come into a category that might be considered abnormal by conventional standards? Supposing the Minister of whatever were overcome three times a week by the desire to dress up as a woman and flirt with long distance lorry drivers. Would Scott maintain that this desire had no bearing on his behaviour on the four days a week that he was free of it? Certainly, said Scoot, so long as he wasn't frustrated and could avoid crushing feelings of guilt. A big if, in my opinion. Scott, with the air of a man about to produce a world class argument, then asked me whether I considered that my own proclivities (taken on their own) would be enough to make me a bad choice for Home Secretary. My sincere belief that they would prevent me running a laundrette with any degree of efficiency, never mind a government office, failed to convince him. Either he must think I'm not telling the truth, or that my tastes happen to be uniquely debilitating.

Unable to reach any sort of agreement on this point, we went on to discuss one curious aspect of the Lambton affair. Whenever a scandal of this sort occurs, the question of national security is immediately raised. If security *is* a relevant factor, and not merely a convenient smoke screen behind which the powers that be can punish offenders for immorality while pretending to carpet them for quite other reasons, we can assume that the various intelligence agencies make it their business to be up-to-date with their information concerning the larger vice operations. This being so, it is hard to believe that I, 'arding, Dawn Upstairs, Steady Eddie, S. Z. Corbett and my friend Scott know at any given time who are London's top Madames, but that those in charge of National Security don't. Either the heads of MI.5 and the Special Branch know less about a matter bearing on the security of the state than I do (which, on the face of it, seems a trifle unlikley) or Jean Horn has been operating for years with the full knowledge and approval of the authorities. Since we can assume the latter, what are they going to do now? Bust her and start up a dialogue with her successor? And if that is their game, shouldn't they acquaint The *News of the World* with the rules? All very puzzling.

* * *

To my dismay, Emma Jane agrees with my friend Scott. She admits to feelings of contempt for her clients, but only in the context in which she meets them. I asked her to imagine that she was once again a secretary. In such an event, I asked, which of her clients would she be able to respect if he were her boss? She thought for a while and then said : "All of them". I found this hard to believe. Stretching the point a bit, I gave her the example of the eminent statesman whose pleasure it was to be harnessed between the shafts of a pony trap and whipped round his estates by a lady dressed as a Roman charioteer. If he were her boss, would she be able to jump to it with a straight face when he asked her to take a letter? "Of course", she said. Would she be able to take him seriously when he appeared in a Ministerial broadcast, reminding us of our National heritage, of the traditional qualities of this Island race, and of the need to pull our socks up during these difficult times? "Yes", she said. The fact that she was herself occasionally overtaken by the desire to fall to the floor beneath another person should not, she felt, lose her the respect of her fellow citizens, until she took to behaving in such a manner in circumstances that the generality might find inappropriate. Shopping in Woolworth, say, or dining out with her mother. Equally, she felt that the eminent statesman ought not to be barred from high office until he took to presenting himself at the House of Common harnessed to his pony trap. At least she draws the line somewhere.

* * *

Wonders etc. etc. This morning there arrived in the post £30 cash, together with a cheery note on House of Commons writing paper, signed by the M.P.! The man must be insane. It seems scarcely credible, at a time when Bert "The Old Grey Fox" Wickstead is prowling around accusing the most respectable people of indulging in sexual intercourse, that an M.P. should be gratifying his unnatural lusts quite so brazenly. I have filed away the note, in case the fool should ever become Prime Minister.

*　　*　　*

Dawn Upstairs and Stella who Stutters have both been turned over by the Law in the last week: Stella who Stutters for drugs only, but Dawn Upstairs for everything under the sun except dumb insolence and lack of House Spirit.

Both experiences seem to have been unusually disagreeable. Stella who Stutters was enjoying a quiet evening at home with her young man One-eyed Charlie, watching television and minding her own business, when without any warning whatever, without even the sound of a footstep on the stairs, BANG! her front door came down off its hinges and there were jacks everywhere. Terrifying. One minute Robin Day and Panorama and the next you're drowning in a kind of instant Drugs Squad. They'd had a tip-off that One-eyed Charlie was in the process of moving a couple of weights and that with luck they'd find it under the sofa. They ripped the place apart, but came up with nothing. Frustrated they resorted to heavy threats. Unless Stella who Stutters told them where the stuff was hidden, they'd cause trouble for her with her mother.

"Go ahead", said Stella who Stutters defiantly, knowing that her mother, a nice old biddy who lives in the country and is, unbeknown to the fuzz, on the firm, was in fact guarding the stuff in her knitting basket and could be relied on to be cool. In the end the fuzz found a tiny scraping at the bottom of the pipe, enough to get them on a possession charge. This is bad enough, since One-eyed Charlie is already on a suspended sentence. And the flat's a write-off.

"They t-t-t-ore up t-t-wo hundred c-c-cushions", said Stella who Stutters, "and all m-m-my b-b-books". Why would anyone have two hundred cushions?

Dawn Upstair's experience seems, if anything, to have been even more unpleasant. She too was sitting quietly at home watching television, when there was a ring on her door bell.

"Who's that?" called out Dawn.

"Only me Darling", said a male voice, so Dawn, supposing it to be a punter, the silly thing, lets in four tearaways from the Chelsea C.I.D.—well-known not to be gentlemen with whom to query the rules. They'd been tipped off that Dawn Upstairs was handling stolen goods and indeed discovered all manners of things that she was unable to account for satisfactorily. As a kind of bonus they found, and confiscated, the little black book in which she keeps the names, numbers and individual foibles of her various clients. For reasons that seem to me obscure, she is particularly worried about this last item falling into the hands of the law. I tried to convince her that she is doing nothing illegal and that it is naive to suppose that the fuzz didn't know she was on the game almost before she knew it herself. The fuzz may be a lot of things, I pointed out, but at least they're not ill-informed about who's doing what on their patch. This failed to restore Dawn's peace of mind and gave Emma Jane the jim-jams into the bargain.

The interesting aspect of both these incidents is that they demonstrate slight modifications in police procedures since Sir Robert Mark took over as Commissioner. In my day, the fuzz wouldn't have indulged in anything so time-consuming or clumsy as a search for the evidence: more sensibly they brought it with them. When they did this to me, I wasn't too bothered. They seemed to me to be nice enough fellows, who simply had this one behavioural tic: a compulsion to plant pot on members of the laity whose life style they thought might be to their taste. How else, after all, are lowly detectives going to get into the houses of their betters, save by coming through the door with a search warrant in one hand and an ounce of pot in the other, which in the attendant confusion they conjure from nowhere with the aplomb of Channing Pollock plucking doves out of thin air? That's as may be, and the point is that neither in the case of Stella who Stutters nor that of Dawn Upstairs was the evidences planted, nor in either case were the arresting officers

susceptible to proffered *doucements*. Perhaps Sir Robert really
has brought about changes, and I must look into this.

*   *   *

'arding came round last night with his friend Honest John the
Thief. I asked Honest John whether the police are less easy to
do business with than hitherto. Yes, he said, the situation at the
moment was terrible. The police were shooting off in all directions like four-bob rockets, he said, not knowing what had hit
them.
   "Sorry", they say, "but we've got to be leary at the moment.
Can you come back next week?"
   Honest John says the panic will continue for a little while, and
then the situation will revert to normal. He says that he has a lot
of respect for Sir Robert, but that the poor fellow has set himself an impossible task. Honest John naturally subscribes to the
view common among his kind (and correct, in my opinion) that
the police are criminals like himself, but with a head start thanks
to their superior organisation.
   I have decided that it is not police corruption itself that upsets
me (I doubt whether honest citizens often get caught in the
crossfire between cops and robbers), but official refusal to take as
axiomatic what has always been accepted by thinking people :
that it is only by their greater cunning and ruthlessness that the
police are distinguishable from the criminals they're set to catch.
That the majority (deliberately misled, admittedly, by the
governing classes) still fail to recognise this, seems to be one of
the most glaring examples of what Harry Stack Sullivan calls
'selective inattention' : the unconscious censorship of information
likely to raise one's anxiety level. Those set in charge of our
affairs rely, of course, heavily on this device, and they back it
up by imposing their own system of unofficial censorship. (The
standards by which they judge information to be dangerous are
interesting; a play or series on television, for instance, that
showed all politicians to be dangerously corrupt would probably
escape censorship; a T.V. series that showed policemen as they
really are, is unthinkable.) The trouble with selective inattention
practised on a wide scale is that when unwelcome information

does manage to break through the defensive system it is likely to cause even greater anxiety than if the censorship had not been imposed in the first place. Were the false assumption that that the Metropolitan C.I.D. are the altruistic agents of a benevolent state, motivated by nothing more sinister than a love of law and order and a hatred of crime, to be replaced by a sounder assumption that they are in fact people engaged like ourselves in raising their standard of living by fair means or foul (and rather better placed than the rest of us to do so) there would actually be a *lowering* of public anxiety every time one of them was caught with his hand in the till. Among other dangers removed would be the probability that Mr. Justice Melford Stevenson will one day die of apoplexy in his own court. Were his Lordship able to operate on the sound assumption that the crooked cop brought before him was unlike his colleagues only in his carelessness at getting caught, the old party might be able to control his indignation and thus live to a ripe old age.

Anyway, the implications of Sir Robert's attempted clean-up strike me as interesting and I think I may try to put together a small book on the subject. I have in mind a collection of interviews with people who have been assaulted, framed, blackmailed, hospitalised and generally done-up by the politzei. The idea of producing a book that requires no actual writing to be done is very appealing. I'll merely have to hunt down various affronted citizens, thrust a microphone under their noses and sit back while they air their grievances. Not only will this be enormous fun, it might also stand as a useful defence when I'm up for living on immoral earnings. "A ponce? Good gracious me, whatever next? Good Heavens no! I'm doing a book about police corruption". The stupidest defence counsel ought to be able to make something of that.

I might start off with Honest John, who certainly has a couple of things to say on the subject. Once, when helping the police of Putney nick with their enquiries he was questioned to such good purpose round the groin and kidneys that he couldn't walk for three weeks. It so happens that the Commissioner's son-in-law, Tim Williamson, is coming to dinner on Thursday with his wife Christina (Sir Robert's daughter) and I shall discuss the matter with him. Better days ahead.

*   *   *

I have scared away, through no fault of my own as far as I can see, one of Dawn Upstair's best punters. A piece of extraordinarily bad luck. Yesterday, while Emma Jane was out, Dawn Upstairs rang to ask whether she could receive a client in our flat, since her own was being used for similar purposes by Pretty Marie. The punter was coming at three-fifteen, and she would arrive at three o'clock, in plenty of time to let him in. Of course she was late, the dozey thing, and he was early, with the result that at ten past three I opened the door to my old school friend Swainston, whom I'd not seen in eighteen years.

To meet an old school friend is a biazarre misfortune at the best of times, but in these circumstances it was a shock to paralyse the mind and bend the knees. I don't know which of us was the more disconcerted: he, shown up as an afternoon gonk, or I, revealed in the unlovely role of sneaky ponce. He certainly took on the look of a man who's sat on a whoopee cushion at a formal occasion, but I doubt if I held up too well myself.

Once the shock waves had subsided a bit, I realised that coming across him in this situation wasn't so surprising. At Winchester, I now recalled, he'd shown aptitude in only two departments: as an enthusiastic competitor in those Duke of Edinburgh type sports, such as throwing things and running up the sides of hills, and as the possessor of a truly formidable sexual appetite. Indeed, his auto-erotic habits had been so remarkable that Cornford—now a history don at Cambridge—had on one occasion tied a cow bell to the springs of his bed. This had tolled out like a summons to a royal wedding within minutes of Swainston's retirement for the night, with the happy result that the whole dormitory had jumped out of bed supposing it to be the breakfast gong. It was perhaps to be expected that his adult lusts could only be held at at a socially acceptable level by occasional recourse to a professional.

I asked him in and poured him a drink, and he quickly recovered something of the *sang froid* that Winchester prides itself on instilling in its pupils. Indeed, judging by the way he struck me quite hard, and more than once, in and around the wishbone—usually a sign of affection among the upper classes—he was rather pleased to see me. Dawn Upstairs arrived, rattling and gasping and waving her arms about, bless her, but, since public school boys get their priorities right, we ignored her. He kept asking me how good old so-and-so was—mentioning names I could have sworn I was hearing for the first time—until he finally got through with the surprising news that my best friend from those days, Pringle-Fisher, has recently had a bad nervous breakdown. This amazes me. I shared a flat with Pringle-Fisher when I first lived in London and he was of a remarkably cheerful disposition. He played squash a lot and never stopped smiling. I daresay there's a connection. Nothing rattled him. He didn't protest even when I filled up the flat with Indian poets, patrician revolutionaries and other degenerates from Cambridge. He was a really happy man. According to Swainston he was rising fast in the City, until he suddenly keeled over one morning on the floor of the Stock Exchange, short squash player's legs akimbo, sobbing that he was at the end of his tether. "Surprised everyone", said Swainston.

A salutary reminder that you can never tell what's going on behind a person's public mask and similar to the case of Thelma: not another stockbroker, but a very capable girl who used to ride shot gun for Sarah Miles. She never took to me for one reason or another and eventually saw fit to write me a critical letter. It was very good, as it happens, a balanced inventory of my various deficiencies, some of which were news to me. I read it and trembled like a dog on Guy Fawkes night. Three days later she jumped out of a ninth story window. You never can tell with people, or at least I can't.

Anyway, Swainston and I reminisced happily on, Dawn Upstair looked more and more bewildered, and it was all quite jolly and boring. Eventually he departed, the purpose of his visit apparently quite forgotten, and Dawn Upstairs threatened to charge me twenty-five pounds compensation. Most unreasonable, seeing as how you can't help where you go to school, having, as I recall, no say in the matter. Anyway, I'm confident he'll come again. If I'm not mistaken, my friend had lost the frank and optimistic look (paradoxically induced by frequent cold baths and being kicked up the arse at an impressionable age) traditionally associated with Wykehamists, and wore instead the rather furtive expression of a man who likes a tea dance. Or so I told Dawn Upstairs. She calmed down eventually, and became her usual chatty self.

"Here", she said, "no, listen. I must tell you what happened last night. Oooh, you should have been there! No, Listen. Me and Eddie only pick up this couple at the Speak, don't we, and bring them back to my place. Well, I'm fancying the fellow, aren't I, and he fancies the chick, does Eddie, she was so *pretty*, it was a buzz just to look at her, you must meet her, and I'm thinking hullo we'll have a scene. Smashing".

"Did you?"

"No".

She is a pleasure.

*　*　*

How call girls spend their considerable incomes provides quite an interesting study. Certain extravagances, I've noticed, are commmon to both classes previously described as unalike. All business girls, for instance, live high on the hog and their fridges are permanently stocked with every known delicacy, from wild strawberries out of season to Fortnum's rarest pâté. They patronise only the most expensive poulterers and struggle home with two or three brace of pheasants at a time. Another common peculiarity is a disinclination to walk any distance in excess of ten yards. Since any form of public transport is out of the question, and since the use of taxis would involve their standing for several minutes on draughty corners, mini-cabs are summoned up for the simplest expeditions.

With Big Elaine, particularly, this habit amounts to an eccentricity. Granted she's a large girl with more to carry around than the rest of us, but her refusal to move one yard in the open air under her own steam is unreasonable, I think. To my certain knowledge the furthest she's walked since I've been in residence has been from the front door of our flat to the waiting mini-cab at the main entrance to the building. If it were possible for a mini-cab to come up in the lift she would avail herself of this service. Furthermore, were you to light a bonfire under her, she would call not the fire brigade but the local mini-cab office and she'd wait contentedly until a car arrived to carry her to safety. Though a thrifty business woman in other respects, she doesn't seem to be aware of the quite exceptional expense entailed by this refusal to budge. The decision, for instance, to buy a tube of toothpaste involves her in an outlay of at least ten pounds. A mini-cab is summoned, and since even she would recognise the absurdity of instructing its driver to convey her across the road to the excellent chemist opposite, she orders him to drive her to a chemist she used to patronise when she lived on the other side of London. After such a journey, it would be foolish to return with nothing more than one tube of Colgate, so she stocks up with every beautifying device currently on the market.

A tart's bathroom is indeed an amazing thing and embodies the only other area of agreement between Big Elaine and Emma Jane. Here they are of one mind. A bathroom should contain, apart from its traditional appointments, every known aid to beauty and hygiene, every spray, rinse, frou-frou powder, shampoo, conditioner, bath salt, bubble essence, herbal prescription, water softener, cream, oil and after bath cologne invented by man. To a cynic who dared to ask whether such lavishness paid dividends in terms of unexampled feminine perfection, it could be pointed out that the disproportion between intention and effect might be even more pronounced were such precautions never taken.

Outside the bathroom, dissimilarities take over once again. Big Elaine, for instance, spends far more on clothes, accessories and props. Seeing herself as a branch of the entertainment industry, an artiste in fact, required in the course of her career to play many contrasting roles, she has an accent to go with each occasion, and an outfit for every accent. Her collection of wigs alone takes up two shelves of her enormous wardrobe, while the blinding concoctions of sequinned, fluorescent material, which she refers to as her evenin' gowns, would in number and style adequately dress the Latin Quarter floor show for the next year.

"My clients", she says by way of explanation, "appreciate a little glamour".

That's as may be, but what can they think when the evenin' gowns come off? Last week I copped her running to the bathroom and I couldn't help noticing, before tactfully averting my eyes, that in the buff she bears a more than passing resemblance to Ian "Mighty Mouse" MacLauchlan, the Scottish front row forward. I must admit her customers seem satisfied, which can only mean that an alternative way of life awaits the "Mighty Mouse", should the rough and tumble of international rugger eventually prove too taxing.

Emma Jane, on the other hand, in accordance with the flip attitudes of her kind, tends to turn up, whatever the demands of the situation, in jeans and a Jeff Banks top. (Jeff Banks would be a millionaire, it seems to me, were he to sell his gear to no-one but the trendier whores). So where does her money go? This is something of a mystery, for go it does, and, unlike Big Elaine's, not into a bank against a rainy day. I estimate, on the evidence to date, that Emma Jane grosses something in the region of £150 per week. This, when one consideres that it's tax free, is a fortune, probably in excess, for instance of the take home pay of a senior executive at J. Walter Thompson. And unlike the executive at J.W.T., Emma Jane hasn't got a wife, three children of school age, two cars, a house in Barnes and a Labrador to support. She has me, of course, but my demands are more reasonable than those of any wife. I never complain that I have nothing to wear (though I haven't, as it happens), weep mysteriously in the middle of the night, demand that I be taken out to dinner because "you never do nice things like that anymore", or, gripped by some imaginary notion that I'm receiving less than the national average in terms of sensual gratification, cause the level of dumb resentment in the flat to rise tangibly like bog mist. I'm pleasant at all times, eat up my grub and evince deep gratitude for such hand-outs as pass my way. I admit, of course, that I'm enjoying a standard of living which normally would represent a net income of sixty pounds a week at least. But that is not what I'm costing Emma Jane. I'm the beneficiary of comforts that she'd be paying for whether I was here or not. In terms of hard cash going into my pocket and never to be seen again, I cannot cost her more than twenty-five pounds a week.

So where does all the money go? So intrigued have I become by this mystery, that yesterday I set myself to computing the matter on the back of a cigarette packet. For security reasons (I didn't wish to be accused again of poking my nose into the running of the family business) I retired to the bathroom and locked the door. Twenty-five minutes later, when Big Elaine banged on the door to enquire thoughtfully whether something was amiss, I had not been able to push the figure in the outgoings column higher than eighty pounds a week. I included every-thing—rent, rates, lighting and heating, hire charges (three

T.V.'s: two colour, one black and white), wardrobe replacements and upkeep, P.R., transport, medical charges (including drugs, prescribed and otherwise), food and drink for two grown-ups and a pussy cat, and a reasonable supply of soft core pornography—and under several heads, to be on the safe side, I exaggerated the expense involved. So: seventy pounds each week contrives to liquidise itself and melt away; there is no other explanation.

This represents a serious problem, if not for me at least for Emma Jane. The only point of being on the game is to amass in as short a time as possible a capital sum large enough to finance an early and luxurious retirement. If Emma Jane, who's now been at it for over a year, were to retire tomorrow she'd have nothing to show for it except a few unsuitable clothes, a sauna bath, a respectable collection of the latest sounds, a sullied reputation and a now chronic inability to get up before lunch time and earn an honest living. Nor among members of the class of call girls to which she belongs is she alone in this respect. Not one of them, I'd guess, is salting anything away. So how can they ever stop? Not, certainly, by finding a suitable man and settling down. Conditioned by the nature of their business to finding any man over the age of thirty-five absurd, it would not occur to them to look for romance outside the field of bass guitarists in unemployable rock and roll bands or pushers on their third suspended sentence. Were an eligible fellow, a man whose qualities of intellect and drive had brought him to the top of the pile, a man whose accumulated wealth was sufficient to comfort and protect the most demanding whore for the rest of her life—a fashionable Q.C., say, or the proprietor of an investment trust—were such a man to present himself as a suitor, they'd look at him in horror, categorise him once and forever as a gonk and charge him thirty quid.

The future is less gloomy, or so it seems to me, for the likes of Big Elaine. For one thing they are not in the least vulnerable to the sulky little rotters who attach themselves like liver flukes to Dawn Upstairs and her sort. They view anyone under thirty as a potential pick-pocket, and after such a person's been to call they tend to count the silver and run a spot check on the contents of their bags. Indeed they are exclusively attracted to what they'd refer to as mature gentlemen, and their dream is of four

and a half acres in Godalming, safely berthed alongside a super-
annuated banker of sixty-six. I doubt, in fact, whether this
fantasy is often, if ever, realised. There is, after all, never a
shortage of competition from younger, prettier and no less ruth-
less amateur hustlers—tap dancers, T.V. hostesses, carnival
queens—for the hand of even the most decrepit millionaire. But
it's a dream that gets them through the day, that sustains them
as they hurtle with the devotion of a blood transfusion unit back
and forth between the Hilton and the Mayfair, and when it
finally bursts, at least they have a sizable nest egg to ease the
pain.

For they earn, by my calculations, about twice as much as
the dotty group to which Emma Jane belongs. And not because
they're more desirable. If anything the reverse might be the
case. In this world, as in the world of fashion models, there is
no correspondence between the physical attributes of the com-
peting girls and the sums of money earned. Just as a top model
owes her bewildering success more often than not to qualities
of industry and cheerfulness under stress rather than to any
noticeable physical superiority over her colleagues, so does a
whore earn more by being patient and obliging. Startling, or
even conventional, good looks are not, after all, what a punter's
looking for. Were he to come across them unexpectedly, he'd
probably turn and run. No, what he seeks is a particular way
of being treated.

Since coming back from Spain, I've only met three business
girls who might, outside the judgement of those already walking
into the furniture, be thought to earn a living from their looks:
Dawn Upstairs, Scatty Sally and Pretty Marie. Both Scatty
Sally and Pretty Marie are outstandingly attractive, ex-models
who eventually found that posing for the soft core porn ads now
to be seen in the *Times* and *Vogue* was a touch too wearysome,
and neither, amazingly, is half as successful in her new career
as Big Elaine. Last week, indeed, Scatty Sally was reduced to
raising a loan from this very source. She came round with the
intention of tapping Emma Jane, but drawing a blank here, she
was compelled to try her luck with Big Elaine. Big Elaine tut-
tutted disapprovingly, but eventually produced from under her
bed a bankroll which would not have disgraced a Mafia numbers runner. Scatty Sally had asked for twenty quid, but Big

Elaine prudently fobbed her off with a fiver. Scatty Sally went off quite cheerfully, no doubt to spend the money on a new piece of personal jewellery for her current boy-friend, a writer at the Great American Disaster.

"These *girls!*" said Big Elaine, after she'd gone. "*I've* never had to borrow in my life".

And no doubt she never will. Each week her account with the Abbey National grows, and if the four and a half acres in Godalming are never to be hers, at least she'll be able to realise her current dream, which is to open a Vietnamese restaurant in the Cromwell Road.

* * *

Tim and Christina to dinner. Lest they depart with the impression that life in a brothel is much like life anywhere else, we arranged a small cabaret for their entertainment. Scarcely had we sat down to dinner, than Steady Eddie (we needed a male voice) rang the front door bell. Emma Jane, looking ill at ease, but pointing out that the dinner had to be paid for somehow, went to answer it and then disappeared into the bedroom with Steady Eddie. After an embarrassingly short time, she re-emerged, said goodbye to Steady Eddie in the hall, and rejoined us at the dinner table. She said nothing further by way of explanation, but handed me a fiver, presumably as my share of the take.

Tim and Christina reacted to all this in a totally unforeseeable fashion. We had expected them to be intrigued, to say the least, and to question us closely. It is not every night, after all, that you go out to dinner with nice people and the hostess pays for the occasion by doing a trick between the soup and fish. In the event, both Tim and Christina reacted precisely as any well bred couple would if their hostess committed a minor social *faux-pas*, such as over salting the irish stew or treading in the *bombe surprise:* they ignored the incident completely and continued to chat of this and that as though nothing untoward had occurred. Only an almost imperceptible tightening up of their expressions indicated a determination to comfort themselves appropriately in these unusual circumstances. And it was not that they were being ultra-cool or that they suspected a candid camera type set-up. It was simply that their breeding had conditioned them to cope with such a social catastrophe in only one way: by politely averting their eyes from the scene of the accident. Extraordinary. I would have expected this reaction from complete strangers, but we know Tim and Christina as well as one can know anyone.

Over coffee and the after eights, I brought up the subject of police corruption. Tim confirmed that Sir Robert, with whom he and Christina took tea only this week, has but two interests in life: an electric carving knife, which Lady Mark gave him for Christmas and which he insists on using even to cut the seed cake, and a fanatical determination to clean up the London C.I.D.

How, I asked, did he propose to do this, except by the rather sensational step of dismissing every corrupt member? An effective measure certainly, but one that would require Sir Robert to police the capital all by himself. Like it or not, he was now a politician and might be persuaded to keep on certain senior officers, for reasons of morale and house spirit.

Nonsense, said Tim, Sir Robert would prosecute without hesitation the person next to him in the hierachy if he knew him to be a rotten egg.

So we have made a bet. If a recently suspended senior C.I.D. officer is prosecuted within three months, I have to lay on Timmy's fantasy for him (in front of Christina he couldn't divulge what this might be), but if he is still at liberty, Timmy has to arrange mine. He thinks that my belief that everyone is as dishonest as myself is possibly mistaken. I pointed out that I don't believe that everyone is as dishonest as me, merely everyone in the Metropolitan C.I.D. I mentioned the matter of Mr. Justice Melford Stevenson's health and Tim pointed out, correctly, that my dislike of the Judge is rather more irrational than the Judge's dislike of young yahoos who hit old ladies over the head. I had to agree with this. I'm against long gaol sentences, except for Judges. This is hardly a rational position. Tim is of the opinion that Sir Melford's sentencing record is not noticeably more savage than his colleagues', but that his Draconian reputation is the result of what a master at my old school

55

would have called an over-developed sense of humour. He's such an accomplished comic, apparently, that he can send a man to the pokey for twenty-five years and make it sound like thirty. Tim then said that he was against gaol sentences except for crimes of violence. I can't agree with this. The prospect of gaol may not deter professional criminals, but it certainly discourages honest citizens—merchant bankers, say or lawyers—from helping themselves too outrageously beyond the limits entailed by the current conventions.

I told Tim of my idea for a book about police corruption and he seemed to approve. He wondered, however, whether a self-confessed ponce would be widely considered to be the ideal editor for such an enterprise. He tentatively suggested that, in order to defuse the inevitable charges that the book is a mere anthology of ravings by cranks and criminals, I ought to collaborate on it with someone notably respectable, like my friend Lord Dynevor. He may have a point here, and next week I propose to visit Lord Dynevor at the lunatic asylum in Swiss Cottage, where he is presently having his head attended to. A wise precaution on his part. "It pays to have your head together", as Black Danielle said last night, and she's right about that and no mistake.

*   *   *

Lunch with Perry, who now has to do with community relations in Notting Hill Gate. He says that his great pleasure, now that he's given up show business, is to lay concrete. It seems that he has been doing a lot of this, particularly in Sussex. Very therapeutic, he says. Can't quite see what this has got to do with community relations, but there you go. His official activities have made him something of an authority on police behaviour, so I told him of my plans. There's a secret force, he says, quite separate from the Special Branch or those uniformed ruffians who drive round armed to the teeth like Franco's bodyguard, who are called out in times of trouble. During a recent affray in his neighbourhood, a large black van drove up and out hopped some twenty of the most alarming men he'd ever seen. They were built like miniature bouncers and each had a Ronald Coleman moustache and a little pork pie hat perched on top of his bullet head. As he watched them go to work, he tried to work out whether it was the pork pie hats or the fact that they were all so small that they made them so menacing. I know what he means, and they are certainly a brilliant invention on the part of the authorities. How imaginative of them to realise that one small angry man in a pork pie hat is twice as intimidating as a lorry load of amiable bruisers. Two hundred such men could take the country over. I must find out more about them and, if possible, where they are kept. I imagine that they are chained up in cages, starved of food, taunted and poked with sticks from time to time by undercover agents dressed up as Blacks, Irish, hippies, pornographers, Bolshevists and other dissident elements. When required, they merely have to be pointed like crazed Alsatians in the right direction, and away they go.

*   *   *

Lunch with Scott. He wants to do a long, in-depth television interview with a call-girl. He is keen to discover what it is that makes such a person tick and clearly supposes that there are three classes of featherless bi-peds : men, women and whores. It seems to me that he is here making what fastidious formal logicians like One-Eyed Charlie would call a category mistake. Like a man who thinks that when buying a pair of shoes he is acquiring three things—a left shoe, a right shoe and the pair— so Scott when dining with me and Emma Jane clearly imagines that he is sitting down with three other people : a man, a woman and a whore. Like a lot of people, he speaks of call girls (not altogether offensively—indeed there is a kind of grudging respect in his tone) as though they are alien beings, outwardly similar to ourselves, but constructed on a foreign planet and sent to Earth to confuse us. Scott didn't go so far as to suggest that there is one, vital, humanising ingredient mysteriously missing in all whores, but he implied it. He clearly believes that intelligent scientific research, carried out by himself in rigorous conditions, would uncover this baffling and unifying defect. I said that a search among whores for a significant common denominator would be as pointless as a similar search among the members of any other profession. A common denominator might indeed be found, but it would be of a negative quality, and its discovery wouldn't get one very far. All policemen, for instance, have in common an *absence* of any innate disinclination to get other people into trouble. Stockbrokers all share an absence of an objection to being stockbrokers. Equally, it could be said of all whores that they lack a woman's traditional inability to sleep with someone they find unattractive, even for money. I do not see that this negative quality makes whores in some way "unnatural", any more than the negative qualities common to all policemen or stockbrokers make *them* "unnatural".

Perhaps one can be slightly more positive, however. For Emma Jane, the difference between not doing something she finds repulsive and doing it, is twenty-five pounds. For Miss X it might be a thousand pounds, for Miss Y a million. It could fairly be said of all whores, I suppose, that their desire for money is greater than that of girls who are not whores, and why this should be so is perhaps worth investigating. In spite of what I said to Scott, I must admit that I can now spot a potential whore some time before she actually becomes one, and probably some time before she herself realises that she is pointing in that direction. If she is over thirty, the task is simple. She will be a casualty of the sex war, a victim of a male orientated society's persuasive suggestion that outstandingly pretty girls should be outstandingly pretty girls and nothing else. Most pretty girls, of course, return from the front line comparatively unscathed and when it is their turn to retire from active duty, they usually manage the transition painlessly. Expensive play things become solid wives and mothers almost overnight. A few, however, retain a taste for the battle and for the spoils that naturally accrue to the victorious, long after the established age of retirement. There is only one way that such girls can continue to compete with younger and now prettier rivals for what they have been taught are the good things in life.

A potential whore who was still young would be harder to recognise. For a start, she would be of only average looks. (A pretty girl of twenty can get what she wants without having to offer herself in exchange). At an early age, she would have discovered that in order to draw male attention away from prettier girls, she had to be more obviously available. As a result, she would, by the age of eighteen, have already slept with far more men than her own desires would have dictated, and she would have discovered that sex without pleasure is not, even for women, the end of the world. Unremarkable of appearance, and without any particular talent or vocation, she would yet have to earn a living. Being by nature passive and unadventurous, she would ignore openings for lady burglars, package tour couriers, interior decorators and petrol pump attendants, and would opt instead for a position as receptionist in an advertising agency. Since she would be totally without ambition and certainly wouldn't see herself as potential executive material, this would be mere labour. Bored to stupefaction eight hours a day, five days a week, it yet wouldn't occur to her at this stage that there might be an escape route from such drudgery. Or if it did, she would assume that it took the form of marriage to an accountant and a two-up, two-down in Edgeware. (Well aware that she is far from being the object of male fantasies the world over, *her* fantasies would not involve fairy princes in Maseratis, or property developers with a place of their own in the Caribbean. They would seem to be the end of term prizes for models, actresses or go-go dancers).

At about this time it might cross her mind that the only accountant of her acquaintance was in fact the rather dull fiance of her equally dull flat mate, and furthermore that it was as much to get away from their stifling company as it was to compensate for the misery of her day time occupation that she was beginning to spend every night in the unsuitable watering holes of unsuitable people, being pulled by all and sundry, from out of work drummers to quite celebrated actors and pop singers.

Gradually she would discover that, although she wasn't a pretty girl, most men—even desirable men—didn't seem able to tell the difference, or if they could, they didn't seem to mind. Having lacked confidence from an early age, she would find this very reassuring. So long as the owners of the strange and luxurious pads in which she would increasingly find herself at day break were, by her definition, celebrities, she wouldn't be too downcast by the fact that they seldom asked her back a second time. Pop group drummers, she would discover to her pleasure, and ephemeral trend-setters of every sort appeared to grow on trees. (That her equally unremarkable flat mate seemed not to need this continual boost to her self-esteem, she would note, but fail to comprehend). Keen to remain a member of this new and attractive mileu, she would naturally come to embrace its values and find those of the world she'd left increasingly irksome. Smoking would no longer be an occasional pleasure, but a way of life, and the procedures, idioms, language and speed (as she'd now call it) of her new environment would take hold of her mind completely. The need to be totally free would seem the most alluring of her new community's tyrannical laws, and, most relevantly from the point of view of her impending vocation, her sexual behaviour would fall more and more into that chic area termed polymorphous perverse. Her day-time occupation would become no more than a vague, semi-conscious gesture, but the strain would begin to tell and after a month or two she would resemble a walking terminal case. Now it would be merely a question of time and chance before she discovered, or had pointed out to her, the solution to her problem. Half the girls who frequent the more fashionable discotheques are whores, and all whores are Madames as well (a fact not fully recognised, it seems, by the authorities). Sooner or later, one of these alert hustlers, ever on the look-out, like talent scouts, for promising amateurs, would spot her vulnerable condition and seek to help her. (It is a common fallacy that girls are introduced to prostitution by sharp-eyed madames and unscrupulous pimps. The majority embrace the way of life at the suggestion of a well-meaning friend, and would scarcely know of the existence of madames and pimps were it not for the *News of the World*). The transition from enthusiastic groupie to full time professional would now be quick and painless, and at first she would hardly believe her luck that she was being rewarded beyond her wildest dreams for doing precisely what she'd been doing for months without any financial inducement. This process seems to me predictable and, I must admit, entirely sensible. I do not see by what other method such a girl could achieve a desirable life-style. The mystery is not why a girl like this is on the game, but why so many aren't. That is the question to which Scott should try to find the answer, and he should interview not a whore, but a secretary.

The life has its drawbacks, of course. An early casualty is her hitherto healthy attitude to sex. Almost overnight she becomes militantly unpromiscuous and her nausea at the prospect of intercourse without recompense with someone she finds unattractive is comical. If you told Emma Jane that she had to go to bed with one of her clients without being paid, she would become physically ill. This doesn't seem to make sense, and at first I used to spend long hours pondering the implications. If you find someone nauseating, twenty-five pounds isn't going to make him seem less so. I now understand that it is not a question of physical disgust, but of professional ethics. A principle is at stake. Call girls, just like any professional class, are geared to the notion of reward. Dentists, barristers, actresses, journalists and plumbers all do things from time to time that are distasteful, and they explain their willingness to do these things by pointing out that: "it's all part of the job". All would be outraged, perhaps even physically ill, by the suggestion that they should do it without reward.

A tart's attitude towards her clients seems to me to be directly analogous to that which psychoanalysts of the T. S. Szasz School say should exist between doctor and patient. T. S. Szasz's position, if I understand it correctly, is that an analyst must on no account see a patient without exacting a fee. If a patient owes money, the analyst must break off the treatment rather than waive an overdue account. If a patient has to cancel an appointment owing to illness, he must still pay up. Without this strict attitude towards money, the analyst might feel himself to be exploited and he might make counter demands upon the patient, to which he has no right. The analyst must feel that he is well paid for his services, and the patient that he has no obligation towards the analyst other than to pay his bill. This strictly cash relationship is seen as more open and honest than other attachments. It seems to me that if one substituted "tart" for "analyst" and "punter" for "patient" in the foregoing, one would have described a call girl's position exactly. So long as a client pays his bill, she is happy to lose her own identity and accept his definition of reality without question. In return for money, she will give him her undivided loyalty, and like a good analyst,

61

never suggest that his wife has a point or that his desires are unnatural. Offering so much, it is perhaps to be expected that she will feel betrayed if someone demands this remarkable service on the national health. (Unlike Szasz, however, she might feel obliged to restrain a client who was about to jump out of the window, but this feeling would probably be dictated by a fear of scandal, rather than professional duty).

* * *

Visited Lord Dynevor in the lunatic asylum. Since he supposed I was tucked away in Ibiza, he looked a trifle alarmed when I walked through the door of his comfortable private room. This won't buy the baby a bonnet, I said, up on your feet, we've got work to do. What sort of work? he asked. I explained that we were going to do a book about police corruption. The definition of a good police force, I said, was one that caught more criminals than it employed. The Metropolitan C.I.D. failed in this respect. Why do you need me? asked Lord D. I don't, I said, I need your title, you silly old goat, to fend off wild allegations that the book is prejudiced. He has agreed to meet me at Earl's Court underground station in a week's time. He really is becoming increasingly eccentric, but I worship him.

* * *

Bit of a row over tea with Dawn Upstairs and Emma Jane. We were discussing business generally and I happened to point out that in these liberated times the traditional function of the call girl was being threatened on all sides. Not only was the competition from Escort Agencies, visiting masseuses, night-club hostesses and uni-sex sauna bath establishments becoming stiffer everyday, but little secretaries were now giving it away in the lunch hour in return for a sandwich and a bottle of pop. To stay in business these days, I said, a call girl had to be a specialist, standing in relation to other girls as a Harley Street consultant does to the general practitioner. They should cater to deviants, and if a client wasn't a deviant when he arrived, he should be by the time he left. He should be taught to believe that only Miss X could solve his special problem and then, since it is in the nature of an unorthodox taste that he becomes compulsive, he would return again and again.

For some extraordinary reason Dawn Upstairs and Emma Jane took this as personal criticism and assumed that I was accusing them of incompetence. Precisely what I was doing, as it happens, though of course I denied it. Both are entirely slaphappy in their methods and neither gives deep thought to a particular client's special requirements. In this respect they are like lazy casting directors. I once put on a prurient, hot-eyed little farce called *From the French*—maggot-rotten with the grubby, nervous jokes by which the Society of West End Theatre Managers, under the morally inspiring leadership of Sir Emile Littler, recognised Family Entertainments in those days, and still do for all I know—and this required a leading man who was a caricature of an ooh-la-la Frenchman, with a long nose, cognac soaked voice and drowsy eyes. I rang up M.C.A.—an agency that was reasonably well thought of at the time—and asked whether they had a mime such as this on their books. They thought for a while and then suggested McDonald Hobley.

Most of Dawn Upstairs's recommendations are as spectacularly wide of the mark. If a punter, taking her to be something of an expert in this department, asks her to supply him with an angry sadist in black thigh boots brandishing a bull-whip, she is quite likely to send little Emma Jane; but if he wants a small girl cuddling a teddy bear, she will probably send German Helga, who looks like Marlene Dietrich's grandmother.

Emma Jane and Dawn Upstairs became crosser and crosser, and finally told me to belt up because I didn't know what I was talking about. But I'm right, of course, and they're wrong. Unless a call girl can build up a solid, reliable clientele of perverts, she will be in the position of a publisher without a backlist, forever having to drum up new business. And new clients whose only peculiarity is that they want variety will go on looking for it. Punters of this sort are better off with Escort Agencies, which nowadays are call girls rings thoughtfully licensed by the authorities. Only two of Emma Jane's clients could be called regulars and both are peculiar to an extreme. The majority want nothing more—bizarre though it may seem—than a straight, though commercial, relationship. That they should be obliged, in these permissive times, to pay for it is strange, as is the fact that not all of them are middle-aged and ridiculous. Some are young and ridiculous. But only two turn up regularly and both—proving my point—are noticeably odd: Nigel the Schoolmaster and The Wanker.

The Wanker is so called not because he literally is (though he may be for all I know), but because of the bewildering sequence of false starts, cancellations and changes of plan that take place before he actually shows up. At first we thought that this performance was entirely haphazard, but a precise pattern has now emerged. We have noticed that he keeps every sixth appointment that he makes. This appears to be a rule, like the sixth tackle requirement in Rugby League. He rings on Tuesday, for instance, and makes a booking for Wednesday tea-time. On Wednesday morning he rings up to say that an unexpected business meeting has cropped up and that he will phone again the next day. This he does, but only to say that he now has to fly to Zermatt for the night and that he'll ring on his return. Back in London, he rings to say that he'll ring again in the afternoon. In the afternoon he makes another appointment for the following day. On this occasion, he actually turns up for his consultation. Our first explanation, that he's a very busy man, doesn't hold. The pattern is too regular. The build-up is clearly part of the fun. But why? This week, I won 10p off Emma Jane because I'd been counting the air-shots and she hadn't. He was due to come at three o'clock on Friday and since this was the sixth tackle, I was confident that the series had reached its end. At two-thirty I had a nasty moment because he rang to say that he was in Jermyn Street and now had to go to St. James's Square to pick his car up. If it had been towed away, he said, he would regrettably have to cancel his appointment. Emma Jane was sure that this was another get-out, but I refused to lose confidence. And rightly, because he turned up on the stroke of three o'clock.

This incident, since money was at stake, was most exciting, and I think it also provided an explanation of his odd behaviour.

I believe he's trying to kick the habit and purposefully puts little obstacles in his path, rather as a man who is trying to give up smoking hides his last packet of cigarettes somewhere fairly inaccessible, but not hopelessly so, in case the compulsion reaches panic proportions. Thus, he deliberately left his car in a place where it might be towed away. When he does turn up, he's as sweet as pie and disappointingly normal.

Which is more than can be said for Nigel the Schoolmaster, who gets his cognomen not from his profession (in fact he won't divulge what this is), but from his scene. He arrives punctually every Tuesday afternoon at tea-time, carrying a Marks and Spencer shopping bag, which contains a newly purchased school girl's outfit: a gym slip, white socks, straw basher, etc. He also brings a carefully constructed script. This, while it changes in its minor details each week, always involves Emma Jane in the role of a twelve year old. What strikes me as eccentric is that the first hour and fifty minutes of his two hour visit is devoted to a script conference and rehearsals. Emma Jane greets him at the door in her civies—playing herself, so to speak—and they retire immediately to the bedroom for a production meeting. The conversation, I'm told, goes something like this:

"Now then Miss Emma Jane, here's the plan for this week. You put on the schoolgirl's uniform and go into the sauna bath. Here's a naughty magazine I want you to be reading. Now, as the sauna bath grows hotter I want you to undress slowly, until you're wearing nothing but the white socks. It's of the utmost importance that you keep them on. After a while, the naughty magazine causes you to have erotic thoughts and you begin to play with yourself. Got that so far? Good. Now, I've been watching all this through the window in the sauna bath's door, and I'll suddenly burst in as though I've caught you in the act. I'm your classics master, you understand. I scold you for being a naughty girl and threaten to report you to your parents. Okay? You become very frightened and *beg* me not to. (This reaction of yours is *very* important and we'll rehearse it on its own in a moment). I'm adamant, but you plead with me, saying that you've learned a naughty new trick from another girl, which you'll show me if I promise to say nothing to your parents. At last I relent, but not until you've taken my . . . er . . . how shall I put this? . . . my . . . er . . . um in your . . . er

. . . hum . . . ah and . . . . er . . . get the picture? Right. Let's justwalk through it slowly once or twice to make quite sure you've got the hang of it. Okay?"

Emma Jane can keep a straight face throughout all this, or so she says, but the rehearsals would blow it for me. A man's fantasies are a man's fantasies, but I'd have thought a day dream would have to be realised more spontaneously than this. I suggested to Emma Jane that she should get into her costume before his arrival and greet him at the door already in character, but this wouldn't go down at all well apparently. Extraordinary. Not that I've got anything against this sort of carry-on. Men are never more innocently employed, it seems to me, than when letting the air out of a dangerously overblown desire. It's what they do the rest of the time that's a worry.

*   *   *

After years of shuffling anonymously in the shadows, it has been given to little Emma Jane and me to topple the Tory Government. Yesterday *The Times* reported that the M.P. with whom she and Black Danielle had the altercation at the Mayfair (*The Times* didn't word it like this, of course), has been promoted to ministerial rank! And today he phoned from his constituency to make a booking for the afternoon!! Naturally I proposed that we wire the place up like a bedroom in a Moscow hotel and I hide in the wardrobe with seven hundred pounds worth of photographic equipment borrowed from my friend Scott. Emma Jane would have none of this, and when I pressed the matter, she burst into tears and said: "I don't want trouble in any shape or form". Extraordinary. In fact her only concern seemed to be whether the newly appointed Minister knew that the minimum price for one girl had now gone up from twenty pounds to twenty-five. This sort of unimaginative attitude is really heartbreaking. If the Prime Minister turned up at her front door with half the cabinet in tow, she'd ask to see the colour of their money before letting them in.

*   *   *

Lunch with my very dear .6 of a friend John Bassett, who used to wear pink socks and play the trumpet, but is now married.

This was rather a bold enterprise, since it involved my venturing into the West End. Couldn't help noticing that all the shows that opened before I went to Spain are still running. A lot of them appear to be starring Kenneth Williams and the reviews on display describe them—enigmatically—as civilised. Very odd. Bassett, who is now a literary agent with Brian Drew, seemed to be rather down in the mouth; creased with strain, in fact, and bent double under the colossal weight of marital paraphernalia : mortages, second mortagages, life assurance policies, medical schemes, school fees and God knows what. (I met Julian Mitchell on the way to lunch and he told me that Bassett has been despondent ever since the authorities at Wadham told him that he couldn't keep a sousaphone in his room). I told him of my plan to do a book about police corruption with Lord Dynavor, and he, taking us to be a couple of wankers, laughed the idea under the table. He revived my spirits, however, with a story that seems to provide sensational evidence that Richard Ingrams is, after all, a sublimated heterosexual. He then cheered me up still further by pointing out that the most you could say for Ingrams is that he's intellectually too deprived ever to make an appearance in Pseud's Corner. Warming to his theme, he went on to trot out the bewhiskered theory that Private Eye is boring because it lacks a point of view. I think that this widely held opinion is utterly mistaken. The magazine's resolute pin-headedness, its repellent assumption that any idea which is not immediately accessible to a fifth form boy at Shrewsbury is only being advanced to pull the wool over the eyes of cretins, amounts, as I see it, to a very aggressive editorial policy indeed, and one which accounts for its success. The stale, comforting, philistine aroma of a minor public school changing room wafts on the breeze towards the nostrils of the Establishment, who are consequently reassured and allow the magazine to continue on its larkish way. This toothlessness is to be regretted. Edited with a little grit (Booker and Foot couldn't take Ingrams's relent-less beeriness, I suppose, and had to leave), it would amount to more than an occasional giggle. I used to think—for reasons that must have seemed cogent at the time, but which now escape me completely—that Ingrams was a mediocre person, only capable of recognising a target the size of Guy Fawkes, and that he'd be just as happy as the games master at a prep school: blushing scarlet at the approach of matron, encouraging the hearties to rag the swots and fingering the boys while supposedly helping them over the wooden horse in the gym. In the light, however, of a fatally revealing item in the latest issue about a lady's vagina, it now seems arguable that he's dangerously disturbed.

Bassett, in common with other so-called friends, showed not a ripple of consternation when told of my present whereabouts and occupation. Not one of them has had the decency to take me to one side for a pep-talk, yet if one of them ended up as piano player in a baudy house I'd be compelled to mark his card. "You're going down hill, dear", I'd say, "For God's sake pull your socks up before it's too late". I'd be terrifically concerned. The sad truth is that either my friends don't give a toss for my welfare or they are merely surprised that it has taken me so long to settle at an appropriate level. In fact there's a third possibility, for which there's some evidence, and this is that they rather envy me my position. But this surprises me most of all. Conditioned to believe that only certain roles—and that of ponce isn't one of them— provide a self-image that is reassuring, I envy them their structured way of life. They seem to be acting out solid, responsibly constructed three act plays, with a beginning, a middle and a decent family funeral at the end; but I'm caught up in one of those gimcrack little revues that used to be all the go: a few jolly, but boneless, moments; the rest catastrophic airshots and embarrassing blackouts.

Pondered this in the bus on the way home. A gentleman can sum up on top of a bus. Something to do with being a few feet above it all, I dare say, and in my case with the fact that the number 22 route goes past so many addresses from which I've made more or less disorganised exits. I dislike the need to play a role. To a pragmatist, believing that to conceive of an object is to conceive of its practical effects, roles, I suppose, are the whole story. Such a person would say that you can only define electricity by describing what it does and that you can only define a cricketer, a criminal, a politician or a judge by describing his function. It follows from this that to avoid being defined one must cut down the number of things one does to a minimum. But them one will be defined, and treated, as a bum. Even a beachcomber with an inherited income would be compelled to play the role of a beachcomber with an inherited income. But it does seem possible that certain roles are less demanding than others. Those which traditionally have a tendency to take over completely can be avoided. Statesmen seem to be particularly vulnerable, and the shock attendant on total loss of identity often causes madness. Lord Hailsham, for instance, like the Queen, manifestly has an historical sense of himself, and is now only able to recognise himself as one in a line of official portraits on a wall in some numinous building. One-eyed Charlie has drawn my attention to the fact that this blunder on Hailsham's part amounts to another example of a category mistake, causing His Lordship to strut the stage as two quite distinct things : as the Lord Chancellor of England, deserving of our respect and awe, and as Hogg the Imbo, at whom all right-thinking people should throw tomatoes at every opportunity. This process, though hilarious to the rest of us, is no doubt inevitable. I dare say Dawn Upstairs herself would become slightly dotty were she to be appointed Lord Chancellor or Queen of England. The knowledge that all over the country school children were reciting "William William Henry Stephen Henry Richard Dawn Upstairs" would surely cause her behaviour to become eccentric. (It's true that High Office didn't unhinge Lord Gardiner, but he's unbendingly sane and, interestingly, was accounted a failure in the role.) Dawn Upstairs, I'm afraid, might begin to speak in vague, rallying abstractions and would consequently be adjudged to have acquired gravitas.

What of the role of ponce? In many ways it ought to be one of the most desirable. It has little public status and as a convenient label at a cocktail party it's pretty much a non-starter. It's self-evident that the only happy horses in the Grand National are those whose jockeys have fallen off. Beaming from ear to ear, they gambol around the course, ogling their friends in the stand and generally being a bloody nuisance to those horses still bent on winning. No doubt they get a bollocking on their return to the stables for failing to take the outing seriously, but this is a price they're probably prepared to pay. Ponces, similarly shed of their obligations, present the same carefree demeanour to the world. Thanks to this role, the surface facts of my life ar better than they've ever been. The grub's good; there are two colour television sets; cash is distributed like monopoly money; nobody harrasses me; I can get all the culture I need from the local library; sensual stimulation is more available than it should be to an old fart; for the first time in my life I have a job that doesn't require me to traffic with unacceptable people. I have no problems.

And this is precisely what's wrong. I accept the theory that it's the innate need to solve problems that gets us from pillar to post, and a ponce's problems are simply not interesting enough. (He's only got one, as it happens, and this, though absorbing, cannot on its own make up for the lack of others.) Or so I concluded as I alighted from the 22 bus. When I got home Emma Jane was doing a trick with a Spaniard, so I dipped into the Carnets of Albert Camus (as ponces will) and immediately had an experience, which if submitted to Arthur Koestler might make me L.P. winner of the week in his strange coincidence competition. The first passage I came across was the one in which he refers to misplaced nostalgia for other people's lives. This fallacy arises, says Camus, because other people's lives, seen from outside, appear to form a whole. Our own lives, however, seen from inside, are all bits and pieces. "Once again", writes Camus "we run after an illusion of unity". I don't think I'm entirely convinced. Seen from inside or out, Bassett's life has greater unity than mine. My goodness, Steady Eddie's has. At least he's been in the same role for fifteen years.

*   *   *

Drama on the floor above. Steady Eddie went missing three days ago and has now been found holed up with, of all people, Dawn Upstair's good friend Pretty Marie.

A frightful rumpus ensued. First Dawn Upstairs put Steady Eddie's wardrobe in the bath and burned it to black ashes. Then she went round to Pretty Marie's house and threw a potted plant through the drawing room window. When Pretty Marie came out to expostulate, Dawn Upstairs caught her round the ears with her Biba handbag. Steady Eddie was naturally too frightened to intervene, so Dawn Upstairs put another potted plant through the kitchen window and then withdrew, feeling much better.

She is now as right as rain once more, having replaced Steady Eddie with Carwash Candy; a much better choice for a relationship in all respects. Carwash Candy is fiercely protective and if Steady Eddie dared to put his nose into this postal district it's the Home Fleet to a rubber duck he'd leave it on his arse.

Not that Dawn Upsairs can't take care of herself. She was round here for tea today, buoyant as a cork now that she feels herself to be loved again, reporting on a conversation she'd just had with a nasty friend of Steady Eddie's, Steve the Stud. Steve the Stud, after the bitchy fashion of ponces, had been letting Dawn Upstairs know how well Pretty Marie was doing and implying that, by moving in with her, Steady Eddie had gone up a couple of positions in the league.

"Imagine", said Dawn Upstairs, "he was sat on my sofa was Steve, rattling his jewellery and that, you know, and he says, all casual like, 'Oh, Pretty Marie's just got two more film parts'.

"Ooh", I said, "Fucking hell! *Two* more! *How ever* many does that make now? My goodness me, how will she be able to fit them all in?" Then I tell him that I'm doing a bit of modelling.

"Really", he says, "how much do you get an hour?'

. "Well, it's so long since I did any modelling that I had to guess. 'Six pounds an hour', I said. 'Oh', says Steve, 'Pretty Marie gets *ten* pounds an hour!' 'Oh no', I said, 'I think you must be confused. She gets ten pounds for a trick, does Pretty Marie, down in Shepherd Market. She must get less for modelling'." Nice one Dawn Upstairs.

Shortly after this, Jenny the Struck Off Nurse dropped in, and she and Dawn Upstairs agreed that the trouble with people like Steve the Stud was a lack of background.

"He's just an East End boy that's done good, right?" said Dawn Upstairs.

"Right", said Jenny. She herself had been educated at a convent in Ascot before becoming a nurse. Dawn Upstairs asked her how she had found herself on the game and Jenny the Nurse said it had been at the suggestion of her husband, a medical student at the same hospital.

"Well I never", said Dawn Upstairs, "that's not what you expect from a medical student".

"Oh", said Jenny, "he was very musical".

* * *

Like any responsible angel, Emma Jane likes, from time to time, to check on her investment; and to this end small accountancy sessions are held once or twice a week. On these occasions, she puts on a special book-keeper's expression, gives a discreet cough and then asks a question framed to discover if and when she can expect to see an emotional return on her capital outlay. The dividends she seeks are not financial, but merely reassuring indications that I'm learning to plan ahead : small signs that by the weight of her investment she is gradually loosening my infantile grip on childhood : evidence that my horror of choosing one of life's many possibilities to the exclusion of all others—my fear, in fact, that Tuesday's decision to be a train driver will stand in the way of Wednesday's need to be an astronaut—is beginning to slacken. Thus she asks innocent little questions, the answers to which will throw light on whether I see our relationship as an on-going arrangement. "Where shall we go for our holiday this summer?" she'll say, or "Why don't you ask your friend Julian to dinner?" (This last is a subtler attempt to link up the past with the future in some continuing pattern). She's persistent, as any investor has a right to be, but, since my terror has always been that I'll find myself in circumstances in which it's possible to predict at seven o'clock on a Monday evening what might happen at eight, she's not making much progress.

I am though. At long last she seems to be coming to terms with the possibility that I know what she does for a living. As a consequence I am now allowed to sit in when matters of a professional nature are discussed and even, as happened today, to become involved more directly in incidents taking place in the home.

Nigel the Schoolmaster rang last night to give her advance warning of an imaginative variation on his customary Tuesday tea-time theme, and when I showed interest she didn't bite my head off. He was bringing with him on this occasion, he said, a nice little girl, an apprentice to a hairdresser, whom he'd recently picked up in Aylesbury. She was as straight as could be, he said, but he was nonetheless confident that Emma Jane would be able to seduce her in the sauna bath. When asked how he could be so sure, he said that it was on account of her sulky mouth. In fact he said it several times, with the air of a man's who's knocked around a bit. "She's got this sulky mouth, you see".

Emma Jane was not prepared to dispute whether a sulky mouth constituted all the proof necessary of hitherto reined-in perverse tendencies, and agreed to take the contract. Before ringing off, Nigel the Schoolmaster emphasised how important it was that Yvonne—for that was her name—should receive no inkling that it was a put-up job. She must go away, he said, thinking nothing but that she had been to tea with another nice girl—as straight as, if not straighter than, herself—who had taken a spontaneous and uncontrollable liking to her.

"Don't worry", said Emma Jane, "she'll scarcely know what's happened to her".

"Well", said Nigel the Schoolmaster, "thats not quite the idea either".

"Oh piss off", said Emma Jane, "I know what I'm doing".

As luck would have it, Big Elaine was out for the afternoon, and this sort of thing being rather my cup of tea, I persuaded Emma Jane to allow me to hide in Big Elaine's bedroom, from which vantage point I would at least be in good earshot of the proceedings. But before I thus concealed myself, I took up a position at the kitchen window from where I could get a look at Nigel and, more importantly, Yvonne, as they climbed out of his Jaguar.

At this distance he bore a remarkable resemblance to Ted Heath (an impression later confirmed by his voice, which had a deep, monotonous, unnaturally resonant quality like that of a chief constable issuing instructions down a loud hailer to a holed-up fugitive : "Now-look-here, do-you-hear-me-in-there—"), but she looked most attractive, being blonde and—mysteriously for the time of year—becomingly suntanned. The only cause for worry was that from this perspective she seemed to be twice the size of Emma Jane, a disproportion that might have painful consequences should the latter fail to play her cards right. (A point not missed by Emma Jane, who, pressed to the window like myself, took a sudden, alarmed intake of breath, like a bull fighter getting his first view of the afternoon's opposition.) Still, the glimpse I'd had was more than enough to inflame the imagination and I found, once in the safety of Big Elaine's bedroom, that, by spreading myself out flat to the floor and pressing my ear to the crack under the door, I could hear most of what was going on. And very stimulating it sounded too, with Emma Jane being more provocative than is her natural inclination, Yvonne giggling charmingly in the face of compliments from such an unexpected quarter, and Nigel the Schoolmaster, by interposing the occasional assinine observation in his curiously amplified voice, showing himself to be less than an expert at creating a helpful atmosphere.

During a lull, he suddenly remarked—lowering his tone a decibel or two in deference to the classified nature of the information about to be imparted—that he had to do with British Intelligence. Judging by her derisive laugh, Emma Jane found this incredible, but I saw no reason to disbelieve him. Indeed he probably owns it. Then, apropos of nothing, he brought up the subject of black holes in space and I began to think: "Goats and monkeys, short of a stroke of luck, such as the fool dropping dead among the cucumber sandwiches, it will be Tuesday week before Emma Jane is able to engineer Yvonne's downfall".

To make matters worse, some peculiarity in my posture seemed to have caused all feeling to leave my limbs, making me suppose that I would be unable to stand up, were the need to arise. No sooner had I become aware of this unexpected affliction than the need did arise, in the form of a sudden and insistent desire to pee. Looking around the room for an adequate receptacle (happily, I could still move my head), I could see nothing suitable except Basil the Black Actor's bowler hat, which was mysteriously under Big Elaine's bed. I cursed British Intelligence, calling him all manner of disrespectful things, until it crossed my mind to ask who was the bigger twit? British Intelligence, who was at least having his fantasy enacted before his very eyes, if at a price, or I, a man of a certain age, nailed to the floor in pursuit of vicarious thrills, paralysed from the neck down, wondering whether bowler hats were customarily made of material which had the property of holding water, and deciding at last that this must be the case, else toffs would get their heads wet when strolling in the rain? I would have risked using the thing, had I been able to move. Since I couldn't, the matter would have to remain unproven.

Emma Jane seemed, in the circumstances, to take an agonizingly long time to get Yvonne into the sauna bath, which was only to be expected, I suppose, bearing in mind the need to make this shift in the relationship seem spontaneous. No good on this occasion the quick glance at the watch, followed by the unsubtle "Well, that's enough of the small talk, get your clothes off dear, I've got other fish to fry before I knock off". But at last she managed the move, and, since a bomb could go off in the hall and you wouldn't hear it once in the sauna bath, this allowed me, without fear of making too much noise, to perform a curious, rather violent, *terre à terre* routine, like an escapologist battling to get out of strait jacket, which eventually had the effect of forcing sensation back into my limbs. On top of which I discovered a flower vase on the window sill, into which I was able to relieve myself.

Feeling better in every way, I was able to take up my position close to the door in time to hear the action move out of the sauna bath and on to Emma Jane's double bed. Enough feminine squeaks and mewings filtered under my door to rekindle the imagination, which, once alight, refused to be doused even by the rather gauche suggestions emanating from British Intelligence. When Yvonne had had enough, she pottered off to the bathroom and shortly cried out from there :

"I say Emma Jane have you got a deodorant handy?"

"I have", boomed British Intelligence unexpectedly.

"God Heavens, have you really?" said Emma Jane, "how come?"

"I never go anywhere without my briefcase", said British Intelligence. "And in my briefcase I always carry my passport, clean socks, a shirt, a change of underwear and a deodorant. One never knows what's going to happen, does one?"

I suppose one doesn't. When they'd gone, Emma Jane reported that Yvonne had seemed well pleased with the attentions unexpectedly coming her way, but I can't help wondering what she really thought. How often does a nice girl go out to tea, only to find herself underneath a small, angry lesbian, while an

75

imbecile from British Intelligence potters about, offering advice and finishing the fairy cakes? Not every day, even in Aylesbury, I'll be bound, and in my opinion Yvonne knows how many beans make five. I don't like the laugh being on our Emma Jane, but if back home Yvonne isn't giving it away for a pale ale I'll eat my hat.

*   *   *

We've acquired another cat, a wife for Bernard, and this time a blue-cream Burmese: a breed of which I'd not previously heard and one, judging by her rather odd appearance, which I take leave to doubt anyone else had either. Bernard fell instantly in love, and their relationship has presented further opportunities for the kind of conversation suitable between a couple pairing. She's called Samantha and has a twinkle in her eye, which makes me think she may grow into a bit of a slut. Bernard, on the other hand, overnight lost all kittenish characteristics, becoming very straight and aware of his marital responsibilities.

"Bernard tells me", I say (having become very accomplished at this sort of thing), "Bernard tells me that he's unhappy about Samantha being brought up in this sort of atmosphere. He's discovered you're on the game and he's frightened his little wife may go the same way. You know how straight he is".

Emma Jane squirms with pleasure. She can't get enough of this.

"Mind you", I continue, "I tell him he need have no fears. She hasn't got the looks".

"How can you *say* things like that", says Emma Jane indignantly, "and in *front* of her too. My little girl's the most beautiful thing I ever did see".

"She's not *beautiful*. No one could call her beautiful. Bernard's beautiful. A bit thick and straight, but beautiful. Like Gregory Peck say. Samantha must rely on her personality. Like Liza Minelli. Anyway, she's told me—secretly—that she would like to go on the game, just like her Mummy, but we mustn't tell Bernard. She thinks he's too stupid to notice, but if someone told him the shock would be terrible, what with him being so straight".

76

Emma Jane is by now in a state of rapture.

"What's she going to charge?" she whispers, so that Bernard can't hear.

"Milk bottle tops", I say. "She'll put them in the bank so Bernard can't find them. Every now and then she'll buy him a little present".

"Then he'll become suspicious".

"That's tru' ".

In fact, cats—particularly Siamese cats— seems to me to be the answer for people who the need to love something just this side of insanity, without the appalling business of being loved back. Children, being neither as pretty nor as amusing, make a poor substitute. Dawn Upstairs has got quite a sweet little girl call Sarah, but she's not in the same class as our Samantha. Dawn Upstairs brought her to tea yesterday, together with Scotch Anna and her little boy, who surprisingly is as black as your hat. They had some story, which I couldn't for the life of me follow, to do with schools and catchment areas, the point of which seemed to be that Scotch Anna has just given our address to the Headmistress of a school in the area, so that her son might attend it. I couldn't understand all this, but in the course of the explanation she did produce a marvellous euphemism for a call girl. She and Dawn Upstairs had just had an interview with the Headmistress of this school and when interrogated as to their occupation they had professed themselves to be "actresses, models, that sort of thing".

"How nice", said the Headmistress. "I hope you don't mind my mentioning this, but I have found that the children of you-er—" she paused to look Dawn and Scotch Anna up and down, "er—*artistic* people, do arrive rather late for class".

Poor soul, in this day and age every other person is artistic, particularly in this area. In our block of flats alone, there are fourteen calls girls, three male masseurs, five air hostesses and a waiter from La Popote. When I'm up for living on artistic earnings, I shall plead insanity and hope for the best.

* * *

Emma Jane and Big Elaine have found a new fulcrum for disagreement. It followed a suggestion of mine that we might buff the flat up a bit. For some time it has struck me as several degrees shabbier than is necessitated by the combined gross incomes of the joint lessees. The suggestion was well received, but the discussion as to choice of colour schemes etc. immediately became insulting, revealing a not unexpected incompatibility of taste extending into matters of interior decoration, as into all other areas. The basic problem is that Big Elaine would like the place to be various shades of knicker bocker glory pink, with glass topped coffee tables, artificial ferns and posters from Benidorm on the walls. Emma Jane, on the other hand, favours elephant shit brown as a basic colour, an absence of furniture except for large floor cushions, and low watt orange bulbs so you can't see who's who: not a bad precaution, bearing in mind some of the ropey types who comes to call. The kinder the light, the fewer the shocks.

I quickly gave up the attempt to reconcile the irreconcilable and fell instead to regretting that I had never kept the sets of old shows. What a waste! Many of them would have made excellent drawing rooms and some would have solved the housing problem entirely. And at the end of a run one had to pay someone a hundred pounds to tow them away to wherever old sets go to die. I feel particularly that the quite elaborate revolve used in *Wham Bam thank you Mam* would come in handy now. We could erect it in the living room and give revolving dinner parties. If one lot of guests were not coming up to scratch, we could revolve them off and a more sophisticated bunch, held in readiness backstage, could be revolved on. Not that the particular revolve I have in mind proved altogether reliable. In fact it let us down rather seriously on the first night. We had flown Oscar Brown Jnr over from America at lunatic expense, and his debut upon an English stage was expected to be an exciting moment of live theatre. There was some silly opening sketch and then Oscar Brown was revolved on singing a rather good song called "Like Wow" or something of the sort, specially composed for the occasion by Tony Kinsay. His reception was gratifyingly enthusiastic, but unfortunately the revolve, having brought him to the required point centre stage, failed to stop and revolved him away again singing pluckily but looking disconcerted. Meanwhile at the back of the revolve, Fred Emney, unable to leg it to his dressing room in time, was changing into his costume for the second sketch, unaware that he was about to be revolved into view of the audience. On he came, a stout, elderly gentleman, hopping on one leg as he tried to get out of his trousers and blinking in the unexpected spotlight. No sooner was he on than he was off again, replaced by Oscar Brown, still warbling away against the odds. The revolve, quite out of control now, achieved this effect thirty two times, at which point it suddenly stopped dead, as though satisfied that it had equalled the number of fouetté's required of the ballerina in Act III of *Swan Lake,* and refused to budge again. I left the theatre at this point and never saw any part of that particular show again. We threw it off the end of Brighton pier eventually, but I wish I'd kept the set.

*   *   *

One-eyed Charlie has drawn my attention to the fact that the drama critics of both the *New Statesman* and the *Sunday Telegraph* have had the courage to point out, in an ex-cathedra tone of voice that is quite unanswerable, that eroticism has nothing to do with nudity. They're perfectly right of course. No doubt certain clever dicks will advance the modish argument that attendance at plays in which the cast disport themselves fully clothed is merely boring, but Marcus and Nightingale, thank heavens, have seen that such an experience can be profoundly corrupting. And where will it stop? I've just counted forty-three entertainments currently running in the West End of London in which the artistes, for no good reason that I can see other than to give the audience a cheap erotic thrill, appear fully clothed throughout. Furthermore, I have no doubt that if one's self-respect were so low as to allow one to visit such a place of entertainment, one might well discover that the audience was fully clothed too. Wake up Mary Whitehouse. And Benedict Nightingale has alerted us to a related danger. Reviewing Paul Raymond's *Royalty Follies,* he says that "the total erotic effect is roughly half what could be achieved by Glenda Jackson in full court regalia, looking at a favourite through slit eyes". Absolutely right. Only a puff could think otherwise. One-eyed Charlie has checked the matter out with his contacts in Gerrard Street and its environs and he's discovered that a packet containing five dirty photographs of Miss Jackson fully clothed currently costs ten pounds, but that a set for which the photographer was shrewd enough to persuade her to pose with her head covered by a brown paper bag is changing hands for as much as twenty pounds. I'm trying to cash in on this perverted craze, but when I tried to sell a copy of the *Tatler* to Lord Dynevor for fifty quid he told me to bugger off.

*　　*　　*

Ever since the incident of Yvonne the hairdresser and her adventures in the sauna bath, I have been on at Emma Jane to ask her back for an encore, but this time with myself playing the part of British Intelligence. Emma Jane's immediate reaction to this request was unco-operative to say the least, and remained so. Get your own birds together you mucky little man, was roughly what she said. I pointed out that this attitude was thoroughly unattractive, not to say immoral, since it implied a willingness on her part to oblige British Intelligence, so long as there was thirty quid on the table, but a flat refusal to do anything for me free. Good Heavens, I said, what sort of girl was she? She would rather not debate the point, she said, nor any other relating thereto.

Bravely, I pressed on. Was it merely a matter of money, I asked, or would she continue to turn me down even if I were able to hustle up the necessary finance?

Yes, she said, she would, and anyway, where on earth would I get my hands on thirty pounds? So naturally I asked her to lend it to me. At this point she advised me very nastily to change the subject or I'd regret it. I retaliated by sulking for three days, refusing to speak to anyone including the cats.

This had such a bad effect on morale generally that Emma Jane at last capitulated. But not with a very good grace. Wearing an exceptionally sinister 'you'll be sorry about this' expression, she rang up Yvonne and suggested that she pay another visit to London. She made it sound as alluring as an invitation to have her teeth pulled without gas, but surprisingly Yvonne was delighted and accepted at once. This show of enthusiasm tickled Emma Jane's feminine (or professional) vanity and her attitude changed immediately. In fact she looked as pleased as Punch, until she noticed my enthusiasm, and then she darkened again. "There's no point in *your* getting excited", she said, "I don't suppose anything will happen". "That's up to you", I said. She snorted derisively. "Me? Why me? Good Heavens, if you want something to happen, you make it happen. Is there something wrong with you, or something?" I was tempted to ask whether this had been her attitude with British Intelligence, but refrained. It would have led us back to the matter of thirty pounds, and this didn't seem to be a very fruitful area. I therefore kept my head and avoided contentious topics of conversation for the next forty eight hours: the time that now had to elapse before Aylesbury Yvonne's second down-fall.

She arrived a little late (in a most attractive fluster, caused by some mix-up over transport) and it stuck me at once that the glimpse I'd had of her from the kitchen window had done her less than justice. At close quarters she was extremely pretty, having the somewhat idiotic, doll-like looks of Brucie's Anthea or Sharon from the *Fenn Street Gang*: the sort than men so often favour and which cause such distress among the ranks of Women's Lib. She giggled most winningly, her legs seemed to be everywhere at once, and her habit of saying "reely" and "utterly" every other word was most disturbing. All in all, her erotic impact was far too alarming to be coped with straight, so within minutes of her arrival, I started rolling joints with the mad devotion of a worker in a munitions factory, and shortly thereafter smoked myself legless. This was, as always, a mistake. Annihilating oneself in this sort of situation merely has the effect of replacing manageable nervous tension with advanced paranoia. In no time at all I had rendered myself incapable of speech or action: a familiar consequence of the sudden inability to judge the real thoughts or intentions of the other people in the room, apart from an uncomfortable belief that they are unsympathetic towards oneself.

Had Emma Jane's attitude been more co-operative, this self-inflicted inability of mine to make a helpful contribution might not have mattered. In good form (or motivated by an accountable profit) she'd have taken a firm hold on the situation, putting on suitable sounds, inviting her guest to join her in a military two-step, and generally looking leery. But on this occasion she'd assumed her truculent, if-you-think-I'm-going-to-do-anything-I'll-later-regret-you'd-better-forget-it expression even before Yvonne arrived, and it seemed all too likely that if Yvonne was to pay a return visit to the sauna bath, it would be I who would have to get her there. Since, in my present condition, it would have been unwise to place bets on my ability to persuade a deckhand on a Norwegian whaler to glance at a picture of Raquel Welch, I felt myself to be rather stumped. I took to glaring sullenly at Emma Jane, hoping, I suppose, that I would thus either persuade or terrorise her into pulling her weight. But she stared back stonily and continued to chat unstimulatingly about such things as the price of meat in Aylesbury and remedies for cat 'flu. Unfortunately, frustrated desire turns me, if not definitivley insane, at least into a condition of diminished responsibility. In such a state, I am, thankfully, only marginally dangerous, since my desires happen (purely by the grace of God) not to be to rape or to cause anyone hurt; but I am in the grip of an unmanageable obsession, and hence become anti-social and absurd. No one knows this better than Emma Jane, and I concluded that she must be trying to tip me over the edge. There was no other explanation for her dreadful behaviour. Good Heavens, this was by no means the first time that we had got up to mischief together. Why had she chosen this occasion to behave like Tweety Pie threatened by Sylvester? The reason lay, of course, in Aylesbury Yvonne's exceptional attractiveness; Emma Jane, after the disgracefully mean-minded manner of her sex wasn't going to have her ponce make an outstanding fool of himself over some little chit from Aylesbury. Consumed as I now was by a confusing blend of moral indignation and sexual frenzy, I yet decided to give her one more chance. Perhaps, I thought, my presence was having a decisively inhibiting effect on her technique. She is not in the least butch by inclination and it was asking too much, perhaps, to expect her to play an unattractive role in front of me. I therefore narrowed my eyes in a moody fashion, shot a long meaningful look in her direction, and retired to the bedroom.

Leaving a room in these circumstances is easy enough; the

difficult part is knowing when to go back again. If you are only away for about ten minutes, there are many reasonable explanations for your behaviour : you might have decided on a sudden to clean your teeth, run round the block, let the air out of your neighbour's tyres, post your pools coupon or make a cup of tea. If you are absent for more than ten minutes, however, your conduct might give rise to curiosity on the part of those left behind. And curiosity concerning yourself is the last thing you wish to instil in them, since you only left the room in the first place so that they might become solely involved in one another. It's a hit or miss business, and if you misjudge the atmosphere, and hence the timing of your exit, you're likely to blow the works. At best they'll think you're rude and at worst they'll come looking for you. If they do the latter, they'll find you spread out on the bed, staring at the ceiling—seemingly overcome like Garbo by the need to be alone—and they'll conclude, quite rightly, that you're barmey.

On this occasion, I retired to the bedroom and tried to work out whether their opinion of me mattered one way or the other. I concluded eventually that it didn't. Emma Jane, after all, must have lost any illusions as to my sanity in this sort of situation years previously, and Aylesbury Yvonne could hardly find me odder than British Intelligence. I decided, therefore, to stay in the bedroom for at least half an hour, at the end of which period I would return casually to the living room. If Emma Jane had done nothing to improve the situation—if they were still sitting primly at opposite ends of the sofa discussing ways of cooking a goose—I would take matters into my own hands. I wouldn't necessarily have any success, but, judging by her behaviour on her previous visit, it would be unlikely that Yvonne would call the cops or have the vapours.

I lay on the bed, having fantasies involving Yvonne, and after half an hour returned quietly to the living room, where to my horror the situation hadn't changed at all. Or if it had, only for the worse. In fact they weren't even talking. Emma Jane had picked up a magazine and Yvonne was playing with the cats. (If a guest hasn't got past the stage of playing with the cats after an hour, a social occasion can be rated a miss in my opinion.) Right, I thought, this is it. Before doubts could gather in my mind, paralysing action, I said :

"Would you care to take a sauna bath, Yvonne?"

She gave me a startled look, which wasn't perhaps so surprising, since, apart from saying how-do-you-do, this was probably the first time I had addressed myself to her directly since her arrival. As a child will sometimes look for reassurance from its mother when asked a direct question like "What's your name?" So Yvonne now turned to Emma Jane for guidance.

"Emma Jane, would you like to have a sauna bath?"

I held my breath. This was the crunch. Could Emma Jane's intentions towards me be so malevolent as to lead her to a perverse verdict? She took an age to answer and I had time to consider the facts. She liked me and, if she was to be believed, desired my welfare. She liked Yvonne. She liked sauna baths. Furthermore she liked turning sauna baths to a use, which, though possibly in the minds of their inventor, is not advertised in the literature appertaining to their sales. No, there was not a danger in the world that she would turn down this request. But still she didn't answer, and in the heavy silence I could hear the clock ticking : often the case when stoned, but unnerving on this occasion, since we don't have a clock. At last she looked up from *She* (a pornographic magazine, in my opinion) and spoke :

"I don't think so", she said, "but you go ahead if you like".

She said this pleasantly enough, but managed, as women can, to mix in some magical and indefinable ingredient, which gave the words an ominous meaning quite outside their normal usage. Those were the words she used, but what they means was : "By all means hit me over the head with a shovel and then throw my weighted body into the Thames, if that is what would give you pleasure, and it is possible that we would remain friends thereafter, but I can promise nothing". Yvonne got the picture and re-addressed her full-time attention to the cats.

An incredible move on Emma Jane's part, the shock value of which had immediately destructive consequences of an unforseeable nature. It so happened that I had accompanied my invitation to the sauna bath with a rather curious circular gesture of the right arm. This had started with the arm folded across the chest and had then opened out slowly in an are of 180°, at which point I froze it, for reasons of my own, so that I stood there *en attitude*, while waiting for Emma Jane to answer. The shock of her reply now caused the gesture to continue on its downward sweep, taking with it a rather nasty standard lamp, which I've many times asked Emma Jane to throw away. The standard lamp crashed on to the coffee table, knocking over the bottle of Spanish red, which, n its turn emptied its contents over Samantha, the Blue-Cream Burmese. She panicked and ran straight into a wall, seeming to stun herself like a cartoon cat. All this had the effect of making Emma Jane laugh, and while I can't say I expected her to cry, I've never found that a Keystone Cops element does a lot for a situation in which you're trying to keep the sensual aspect uppermost. In fact I'd go so far as to say that if you want to give up sex, comedy is the most effective aversion therapy.

There didn't seem to be much point in hanging around, so without offering to clear up the mess, I returned to the safety of the bedroom. There is a great peace to be drawn from total failure. I lay on the bed, comparing British Intelligence's deft performance with my own, and after a while I fell asleep. When I woke up, I was surprised to discover that I had slept for two hours. What was going on? Had Yvonne left? I considered the possibilities carefully. No, I decided, she couldn't have done. Her departure would have woken me and anyway Emma Jane would not be sitting alone in the living room. So, if Yvonne was still here, what were they doing? I thought about this and my heart started to beat uncomfortably. Extraordinary. Two hours before, I had decided that no prospect could ever arouse my erotic interest again. I got off the bed and crept into the hall. The sitting room door was closed, whereas before it had been open. Funny. Why would they close the door? My palpitations were now of a strength to make me fear I might keel over, but I decided to risk a heart attack by peeping through the key hole. No go; the key obscured any view of the room. What should I do now? Risk making a fool of myself again by bursting in, or return to the bedroom and there divert my mind into areas of ontological speculation? A silly question. In such circumstances I'm a fanatic, and I began to open the door with incredible slowness, millimetre by millimetre, doubled up still in the key hole position, on the theory that, unless you live with midgets, you don't expect to see heads coming round doors a mere three feet off the floor. I had opened the door about four inches, I suppose, and was on the point of squeezing the right hand side of my head through the crack thus formed, thinking to myself "my hat, this will be good" when I was goosed unexpectedly from the rear. I jerked upright with surprise, catching my head nastily on the door nob as I did so, and spun round to confront my assailant. It was Emma Jane, overcome once more with inappropriate mirth, and—I was quick to spot this—naked.

"Hullo, what's your game?" I said crossly, as though it was her behaviour that called for an explanation.

"*My* game? What's *your* game more like, peeping through key holes in your own flat! Really!"

"You haven't got any clothes on".

"I'm aware of that".

"What were you doing?"

"Making a cup of coffee, as it happens, do you mind?"

"No of course I don't mind. Why should I mind? What a bloody stupid question. Where's Yvonne?"

"She's left. She had to go back to Aylesbury".

"Why are you without your—er—clothes?"

"Why do you think?"

"Did you—er—um—?"

"Yes, of course".

"You—you—" I became incoherent with rage. "Why didn't you—er—you know, er—wake me up?"

"Wake you up?"

"Yes".

"What! You mean I should have said 'Oh, hang on a minute, hold everything, I've just got to go and wake up my old man. He's a bit odd and likes to be present.' It's not my fault if you smash the furniture, frighten the cats and then creep off to the bedroom in a sulk".

"Don't call me odd".

"Well, you are odd, bloody odd. You're a pervert".

Naturally I hit her at this point, not too hard, no more than a crisp tap really, but enough to rock her back on her heels. Then we were at it. The coffee table went for six again, a heavy onyx ashtray winged across the room like a discus, narrowly missing my head, but scoring a direct hit on the standard lamp, which crashed to the floor like a guardsman for the second time in the evening, and before I could fall on top of Emma Jane, smothering her under me in the way that one might throw a blanket over a demented ferret, she fetched me a nasty one behind the right ear with a sparklet soda water syphon.

A very ugly business, and though it goes against the grain to admit it, I do wonder at such times whether there isn't something to be said for being a gonk. Compare British Intelligence's experience with mine. One Monday afternoon he is sitting in his office, wondering whether to hop round to the Chinese Embassy and stuff rice pudding through the letter box (or whatever British Intelligence get up to on a Monday afternoon) when he becomes uncomfortably aware that thoughts of confounding the commies are being insistently pushed to one side by an image of Aylesbury Yvonne going the wrong way in a sauna bath. Does he have to brood and fret over this image for days to come, so that his work suffers and his wife becomes neurotic? Not a bit of it. All he has to do is invest four pence in a phone call to our Emma, and he can sit back in the knowledge that within twenty four hours he will, thanks to her ministrations, be back on the straight and narrow, and able to attend to matters of National interest. The next day, for the outlay of a mere thirty pounds (probably drawn from a British Intelligence fund set up for this very purpose) his desires are reduced to manageable proportions for at least another week. I, on the other hand, seized by desires of a precisely similar nature, am immediately involved in a three day period of ill-natured brooding, followed by a shorter episode of surpassing embarrassment, which inevitably erupts into downright violence, before levelling off into a further forty eight hour period of sullen resentment and mutual mud-slinging, in the course of which, I, who slept with the innocence of a babe while practices of an unnatural kind were taking place next door, am called a pervert. Incredible. It's safer and less time consuming to slap the thirty oncers on the table and cut out the aggravation. I'm sure Mrs. British Intelligence would be the first to agree.

* * *

From the age of four, I have felt myself to be vis-a-vis women, basically in the shit. In all close dealings with women—a nanny, a mother, an elder sister, a wife or a lady friend—I have taken her word for it that the authority to validate reality within a male/female situation has been given to women by God. Men have a purpose, but they don't know how to behave. Or at least I don't. That my behaviour falls some way short of the required standard, I have always taken for granted. Sometimes I have been able to claw my way up into a position of temporary favour, but incapable of comporting myself decently at this level, I have been returned quickly to the dog-house. Two things have recently combined, however, to make me question my basic assumption —the assumption that in any altercation with a woman I'm necessarily (that is to say, by definition) in the wrong. First, all my friends report that they too stumble forward, weighed down by an awful knowledge of their own inadequacy, heads bowed in expectation of some well earned bollocking. This discovery on its own doesn't get us very far. We could all, as a sex, be necessarily in the wrong all the time. But the second discovery is more interesting. This is that, in the course of my relationship with Emma Jane, it has struck me more than once that *she* is in the wrong, or at least might be. At first I couldn't accept this. If she appeared to be in the wrong, this was only a further proof of my moral deformity. Recently, however, certain aspects of her behaviour have caused me to question—rather nervously at first, alarmed by this step into unknown regions—whether her concept of a relationship is necessarily the only valid one.

I don't understand mathematics, but I gather that if one collection is part of another, the one which is a part has fewer terms than the one of which it is a part. The maxim is true, I believe, of finite numbers. The collection of cucumber slices in a salad, for instance, must have fewer terms than the salad of which it is only a part. As far as relationships go, Emma Jane doesn't hold with this notion at all. I would have thought that, in the case of two people sharing, the sum of their combined talents, interests, virtues and abilities was greater than the sum of their individual talents, interests, virtues and abilities. Furthermore, I would have thought that this concept of increase might work to their advantage in the battle for survival and might even cause them to have a more stimulating time together. Emma Jane doesn't agree. Dissimilar virtues and interests are, in her opinion, mutually destructive and must therefore be abandoned. I and You are Involved (an alarming image of entanglement in barbed wire comes to mind) and have become Us. Us struggles on, a hopelessly handicapped assembly, like a couple in a three-legged race, able to compete with other similarly handicapped couples, but left standing by unimpeded individuals.

The worst blasphemy within a Relationship, then, is the notion of disagreement, and this being the case, it follows that a totalitarian system of censorship must be imposed. All subjects on which differing opinions might be held are taboo. On the face of it this would seem to exclude just about everything as a possible theme for discourse, but I must admit that there is a kind of hierachy of banned subjects, and the punishment for touching on certain of them is less severe than is the case with others. Thus, I am permitted to talk for ten minutes on a current obsession (police corruption, say), for five minutes about some matter that's aroused my interest on T.V. (so long as it doesn't involve another subject on the Index), for three minutes on the curious composition of the English football team, for two minutes on One-eyed Charlie's criticism of Popper's solution to the problem of induction, for one minute on Laing (a very dangerous man) and not at all about relationships in general and our relationship in particular. (Interestingly, there is no reciprocal agreement. Refusal to discuss subjects appropriate to a relationship—summer holidays, new curtains for the sitting room, the winsome behaviour of babies, the moral lapses of other women's men—is also a crime.)

Men have to be told, and I made some frightful blunders in the early days: blunders for which I was rightly reprimanded and punished. Repetition of the same blunder entailed a period of solitary confinement, rather as persistent defaulters in *Cool Hand Luke* were played in the Box. After a while, I was myself able to tell when I had committed a gaucherie of the first magnitude and on these occasions I went straight into the Box without having to be told. This saved time and trouble. More recently I have acquired a certain decorum and generally manage to suppress behaviour likely to be construed as a breach of discipline. Sometimes, however, I am unsuccessful. An idea occurs to me, and though I recognise that it has to do with a banned subject, I cannot control myself. Like a man fighting down a social faux-pas after eating a plate of radishes, I struggle hard against the need to communicate it, but it won't be contained and it escapes inevitably like wind.

Precisely this happened today. Two items in the Sunday papers caught my eye today, and though I knew it would lead to tears, I was compelled to draw Emma Jane's attention to both of them. The first was a quote from Diana Rigg in which she said : "For thirty five years I've lived as I wished, with whom I've wished, in the manner which I wished, and it's curious how a lack of definition led me in the end to want to adhere to something. I came round to the belief in living with one man in a state of marriage".

I thought this was funny (whether intentionally or not, I don't know) since it can only mean that marriage for Miss Rigg has involved her in living with someone with whom she doesn't wish to live and in a manner in which she doesn't wish to live. Emma Jane's vinegary expression indicated that she considered this to be a cheap and subversive observation on my part, designed to bring the state of marriage into disrepute, and I would have done well to shut up at this point. However, like a Japanese suicide pilot bent on self-destruction, I pressed on crazily to the second item. This was a review by Anthony Storr of *The Second Sin* by T. S. Szasz, a book in which he apparently discusses human relationships in terms of power politics rather than in terms of love. I even went so far as to read out a passage quoted by Mr. Storr, in which he says : "the spirit of modernity has put love above dignity, the desire to be loved above the desire to be respected".

Even I could see that this was pretty inflamatory stuff, since "love" is Emma Jane's department, not T. S. Szasz's, and certainly not mine, so I didn't dwell on it, but hurried on to another aphorism which interested me still more. This was : "men love liberty because it protects them from control and humiliation by others, and thus affords them the possibility of dignity. They loathe liberty because it throws them back on their own abilities and resources, and thus confronts them with the possibility of insignificance".

Call girls, it seems to me, are greatly confused by this conflict. A desire for freedom (moral as much as financial) is precisely what causes most of them to cancel their membership in the social enterprise in the first place, but having done so, they become frightened of the liberty they have achieved and try to get at least one foot back within the fold. They are forced to maintain a double standard and thus become neurotic. In this respect they are quite unlike criminals, or even hippies, both of which groups are truly liberated in the sense that society's approval has become irrelevant. While call girls vary as to the degree of re-assurance each needs that she has not strayed from the flock beyond any hope of recall (from Big Elaine, who strives for total respectability, at one end of the scale, to Emma Jane, who merely needs a normal—i.e. defined as such by society—emo-tional life, at the other), I've not met one who is entirely free.

Anyway, I drew Emma Jane's attention to these rather un-spectacular observations, whereupon she burst into tears and ran sobbing to the bedroom. Now, the point is that my crime (a serious one, meriting four hours in the Box) consisted not in my having these thoughts, but in communicating them to her. As she herself said when we were once more on speaking terms : "Why do you have to say things that you know will upset me?" I can *think* things that would upset her (this is inevitable, since men are incapable of decent thoughts), but I must on no account put them forward as reasonable topics for discussion. This ban extends, interestingly, to statements whose truth content she is compelled to recognise, with the strange result that the tradi-tional slogan has become : "I agree with with you say, but I will oppose until death your right to say it". Thus, she knows she's a call girl, I know she's a call girl, she knows that I know, but, since in the original Relationship in the sky the woman is not generally supposed to be a whore, nor the man a ponce, a blanket of silence must descend on this awkward defect in our earthly copy. Her position is summed up in the simple syllogism : no relationship between a whore and a ponce is good; I am a whore and you are a ponce; therefore our relationship is not good. This is certainly valid, and since she takes the minor pre-miss to be true by definition and the major premiss to be true by Authority, she has argued herself into an unacceptable con-clusion. Unfortunately, I cannot point this out to her(or attack the truth of the major premiss) since to do so would be a further infringement of the code.

*   *   *

I don't believe it is yet an established orthodoxy that a degree of mental instability is necessary condition of advancement, though One-eyed Charlie tells me that the theory is receiving serious attention in some reputable circles, with special reference to schizoid characteristics. (Certainly the term "mad" would no longer seem to have a useful meaning in a vocabulary that would have described the late Lord Chief Justice Goddard as "sane".) In a rather more serious context, however, the theory does appear to receive confirmation from the behaviour of call girls. There is no doubt, it seems to me, that the more they appear to have lost touch with what would currently be defined as reality, the more successful they are in their chosen profession.

This law applies most noticeably in the case of black call girls, nearly all of whom make spectacularly successful hustlers. Take Black Danielle. She popped in last night and as usual I had to remind myself that she was not under the influence of some hallucinatory drug, but that this was how she normally reacted to her environment.

She is ususual to a marked degree. Blessed by nature with the imposing measurements of a Watusi security guard, she yet seems fearful that anyone under seven feet tall will be at a disadvantage when dealing with cunning, metropolitan Englishmen; accordingly, she adds an extra six inches at one end with an Afro hair-do the size of one of those mines that occasionally beached themselves during the war (she sticks knitting needles into this to guarantee the spikey effect) and, at the other, heels the height of circus stilts. Still not certain, it seems, that these proportions on their own will have the desired impact, she customarily adorns them with clothes of a military motif : war office issue long johns, Luftwaffe surplus great coats and cavalry twill jodhpurs. In case men should find this an irresistible ensemble, she announces at the start of any social occasion, in a voice like two Doberman Pinchers having a misunderstanding, that she is the newly elected London representative of the Dyke-Separatist Movement and cannot abide to be touched by the opposite sex. Fair enough, and the only cause for surprise is that after just twelve months on the game she already has a freehold house in her own name, a Mercedes Benz (though she can't actually drive) and a guaranteed net annual income of ten thousand pounds, subscribed jointly by a gentleman from the Midlands who makes ploughs and a Mayfair art dealer. A certain disproportion between this sort of success and what she has to offer is a source of some bewilderment to her colleagues, but all black call girls seem to me to embody a similar disproportion, and I think there is a ready explanation. It lies, I would say, in a lethal combination of unquenchable optimism and sheer *intention*. To see a black hustler on the job is an enlightening experience. Whereas white girls creep into a room looking suspicious and cross ("I may be a whore", their pinched expressions seem to say, "but no one's going to make a monkey out of me"), a black girl bounces in, beaming from ear to ear, exuberance incarnate, recounting tall stories of the night before and issuing information about the fun to come. Bewitched by such a show, white punters leap from the wheel chairs to which their crippling inhibitions have hitherto confined them, and start to dance around the room. "My goodness, gracious me", they think, "it's all about to happen".

In fact nothing happens at all, or if it does its thanks entirely to the sour faced white girls, who gloomily do their stuff after the black girl has mysteriously departed, having suddenly remembered another even wilder scene she simply must attend. (Black girls, I'm told, have a paranatural ability to extricate themselves from compromising situations seconds before being called upon to lose their clothing. Like manically cheerful warm-up comedians, they take it as their function merely to establish an appropriate atmosphere, and this done, they scarper, leaving to others the responsibility of carrying the show to success. Since it is their self-imposed duty to draw the customers' attention to the considerable charms and abilities of those who will be doing the actual entertaining, they gloatingly disrobe the white girls, breathing heavy compliments the while, which the dopey white girls fall for, too flattered to notice that they're being set up like so many lots at an auction. This done, they hop it fast, safe in the knowledge that the white girls are now in no position to pursue them down the corridor screaming imprecations). Infuriatingly for the white girls, who have done all the work, the punter retains no interest in them, but, mesmerised by the black girl's ability to combine promises of Borgian lubricities with total elusiveness, invests heavily in her direction as a down-payment against astonishments to come.   ·

The black girl is able to get away with this sort of thing because of her childlike conviction that she will do so. She inhabits a magical dreamworld, in which to conceive an ambition is to achieve it. Since she never actually takes the first step towards realising her more outlandish fantasies, her faith remains unimpaired. Last night Black Danielle suddenly said, quite seriously: "I'm thinking of going to the States. I'd like to have my own chat show on T.V. there. I enjoy chatting to people, know what I mean? I don't know though, I suppose it might be a bit heavy. I'll have to think about it".

Then she said: "I might stay here and write a column for a newspaper. I met a columnist last week and he says it's a gas. On the other hand, columnists probably don't get much bread, so perhaps I won't. What do you suggest?"

I suggested that she go to the States, since over there she could have her own T.V. chat show, write a column and have time over to become a film star.

"Oh no", she said, "I thought of being a film star, but I decided against it. Too much of a hassle".

They're not so daft though, these black hustlers. At one point I asked her whether she knew my old friend Daisy Mae from Trinidad.

"Which Daisy Mae do you mean?" she asked. "The original Daisy Mae or the present one?"

I said I was only aware of one, whereupon she roared with laughter. Apparently 'Daisy Mae' is not so much a name as an 'activity' or 'office', and it is passed around among black girls (or rather sold to the higest bidder), because of the goodwill accuring to it. It is the same system, I suppose, as that under which a Publisher, say, will sometimes purchase the imprint of another to acquire its excellent back-list. There exists an agreement whereby only one Daisy Mae can operate at a time, just as there can be only one Warden of the Cinq Ports or Lord Privy Seal, and I suppose that if a rogue Daisy Mae crops up, she either has to change her name or mend her ways. Call girls who want to retire often sell their phone numbers for a considerable sum of money, but I've never before heard of a complete identity changing hands. It's been possible in this case, it seems, because Caucasian gonks can't tell one black girl from another and because the prototype Daisy Mae created a marketable legend. Black Danielle says that there have been five Daisy Mae's to-date and that the business is currently valued at six thousand pounds. I wonder which Daisy Mae I knew. I'm sure she was the original, but apparently everyone thinks this.

*   *   *

One-Eyed Charle has read *Conundrum* by Jan Morris and reports that he has now undergone a colour change. His soul, he insists, has been black since birth. He now likes to be addressed as "brother" by fellow blacks and is offended if the police fail to assault him on sight. An unusually Cartesian stand for a follower of Ryle to take.

*   *   *

There seems to have emerged in the last few years a new and frightening class of self-appointed arbiters in all matters relating to morals and aesthetics. They call themselves "ordinary mothers" and they write to the newspapers and ring up T.V. phone-in discussion programmes, *drawing attention to their ordinariness,* as though it were unanswerable proof of the expert nature of their testimony. Having got Robin Day or Ludovic Kennedy on the line, they say "Hello, I'm just an ordinary mother and ———", at which point you'd expect Mr. Day or Ludo to chip in with "well buzz off you silly old tart and leave the line clear for some informed opinion on this very important topic".

But not a bit of it. Ludo puts on a particularly respectful expression and listens most seriously to a lot of dangerous balls about the collapse of traditional values. Now I read with alarm that these ferocious women have formed themselves into a society called "Mothers in Action." An obscene picture presents itself of platoons of marching women, their good, kind faces aglow with Christian love, as they scream for the immediate return of every sort of lewd violence that a state can visit upon its members.

A much admired speciality of these ladies is their courageous willingness to 'stand by' some member of the family who has committed some minor social faux-pas. When Miss X, for instance, is gloatingly exposed as a leading blue film artiste by the *News of the World* (the information having come from one of their reporters, who also happened to be Miss X's personal manager) her mother is photographed at her side, above the grim quote: "of course I will stand by my daughter. Any ordinary Mother would do the same". Are we to infer that Miss X's ordinary Father has already changed his name, sold the family trinkets and fled in shame to South America? I believe we are.

All this is prompted by the behaviour of Emma Jane's Mother, which is very odd indeed, and to which I naturally give a great deal of thought. She now lives with her husband, the retired Sea-dog, on the coldest part of the Norfolk Coast, but this doesn't prevent her making occasional unscheduled swoops upon our nest, shredding our nerves for days to come. (Sometimes she gives us about half an hour's advance warning, in which event we go to work with the frenzy of alerted speakeasy-proprietors in the days of prohibition). Such a brisk woman would alarm me in any context, but living as I am off her youngest daughter's artistic earnings, it is all I can do not to tremble visibly in her presence. That she hasn't twigged what's going on seems to me inconceivable.

Consider the facts. She's not a vague or dozey lady, but on the contrary as smart as a whip, and it is manifestly from her that Emma Jane has inherited supernatural deductive powers. From the moment little Emma came to live in London, she kept herself closely informed as to her daughter's every movement. It could even be said that she was in all departments an over-conscientious Mother. Was Emma Jane eating sensible meals, mixing in sensible circles, earning enough money, saving her money, keeping warm, thinking ahead? She demanded answers to these questions, and if they were not forthcoming, she put on a sensible hat and drove to London in the family Rover to see for herself. Such a woman could hardly fail to notice that on or about a certain date Emma Jane gave up honest employment and that this premature retirement coincided precisely with a quite remarkable up-surge in her standard of living. Overnight, the mousey little secretary with two dresses, a bagful of luncheon vouchers, a hair dryer that didn't work, a boyfriend in Market Research and a Roman Catholic flatmate who worked for the Electricity Board, had turned into a well-heeled slut, with two colour televisions sets, hi-fi equipment that made the sitting room look like a pirate radio station, a wardrobe full of unlikely £60 creations, a healthy complexion for the first time in her life and a flatmate who couldn't be mistaken on a foggy night at a hundred yards for anything other than what she was.

What, one asked oneself, could an Ordinary Mother be expected to think? Interestingly, it was precisely at this moment, according to Emma Jane, that her Mother abruptly broke off her continuous Gestapo-style snooping and entirely ceased to question her as to the details of her life.

"How", I asked Emma Jane, "do you suppose your Mother accounts for the remarkable improvement in your material well-being, accompanied as it is by a weight of evidence to the effect that for the first time in your life you are not in receipt of a respectably acquired salary?"

"Oh", said Emma Jane, "she probably thinks I've got a rich boyfriend".

Now, this theory is manifest nonsense for two reasons. First, Emma Jane's Mother is not the sort of woman to allow a rich boyfriend to participate in her daughter's arrangements, without making searching enquiries herself as to his name, rank, connections, colour, hat size, religion, political persuasion, profession, prospects and intentions. Secondly, had the rich boyfriend theory held for two minutes, it certainly couldn't have survived, the sudden arrival on the scene, like a nasty wasp zeroing in on a jam jar, of a living-in, impecunious, middle-aged, unemployable lout like me. No, it all adds up to another outstanding example of selective inattention: an Ordinary Mother's ability to impose a rigid system of censorship on all information pointing to the fact that one of her children has gone ever so slightly off the rails.

Or so I thought until recently. Following a weekend visit to Norfolk, I'm not so sure. The alarming thought has occurred to me that it is perhaps I who is suffering from selective inattention, not Emma Jane's Mum. The weekend was pretty heavy going, since it required seventy-two hours of unrelieved role-playing on our part (I did a kind of eccentric schoolmaster of unexplained means and Emma Jane a kitten in love, which was fairly sickening) but there is no denying that her Mother went miles out of her way to be cordial towards me. The sea-dog, it's true, eyed me suspiciously from time to time, but sea-dogs usually do, and he didn't actually say anything. In fact he didn't say a single word all weekend except "Ah, I see the sun's over the yard-arm, permission to open the bar, Betty?", and he only said that at six o'clock in the evening. In an effort to draw him out, I told him of my own experiences in submarines (particularly of the time our captain blew a torpedo out of the wrong end of the boat by mistake, so that instead of proceeding harmlessly out to sea, it hit the Isle of Wight, passing between a surprised couple having a picnic on the beach and causing an argument as to what was in the sandwiches) but he didn't seem very interested.

Betty, on the other hand, (not that I'd dare call her Betty if my life depended on it) was so damned nice to me, so determined, it seemed, to show that she approved of me and whatever my arrangement might be with her daughter, that this new theory began to form itself in my mind. It now seems to me perfectly obvious that Emma Jane's Mum has known all along that her daughter is a whore and lives in terror that I may find out the ugly truth. Rightly seeing that her daughter's only hope of salvation lies in a good, kind man like me, her one fear is that I will suddenly see through whatever cock and bull story she may have fabricated to explain her startling earnings and that I will walk out, shocked and disgusted, taking with me Emma Jane's only chance of happiness. Only selective inattention on my part blinded me to this correct interpretation of her Mother's behaviour.

*   *   *

I have decided to abandon my courageous exposée of police malpractice. For one thing, my collaborator Lord Dynevor has become increasingly unreliable. This may have been brought about by the fact that when discussing the idea with friends he has consistently come up against a reaction of strangulated outrage, manifesting itself in symptoms of imminent explosion. Since Lord Dynevor still moves from time to time in circles where the peasants bed down with the cows, while their employers attend meetings of the Flat Earth Society, this reaction is not so surprising. But it's having a bad effect on his health. Last week he visited his doctor, who diagnosed two hernias, diabetes and a degree of mental instability. Lord Dynevor got the ensuing appointments with various specialists hopelessly muddled, with the result that he took a sample of his urine to his new psychiatrist. The psychiatrist thought he was not a serious person and threw the old fool out.

My real reason for abandoning the project, however, is that I've hit on an idea that interests me more. This follows a visit from a very enthusiastic lady called Anna Raeburn, who works for *Forum* and who seems to have discovered a way of widening her circle of interesting acquaintances that is even more effective than that used by the Drugs Squad. Instead of breaking down the front door of those with whom she thinks it might be pleasant to pass the time of day, she rings them up first and asks whether she may come and talk to them about sex. Few are going to turn down this suggestion, and I certainly didn't.

She is writing a book about group sex, if you please, and since I know nothing about this subject and am not particularly concerned to find out more, I didn't give her a chance to explain her thesis. Instead, I took the opportunity to work out—on the spot so to speak—my new theory concerning Full Frontal Nudity and Simulated Sex Acts as they touch upon the popular arts.

I have always taken the view that either one or the other, or preferably both, could hardly fail to raise the spirits, whenever, or however, it, or both, cropped up in a piece of Family Entertainment. Recently, however, I have been persuaded to a different point of view by the excellent arguments put forward by Ian Robinson in his book *The Survival of English*. Their thrust is, roughly, that since we live in a society in which the convention is for modesty in sexual matters, it follows that nude lovemaking on stage or screen disastrously interupts the artistic rhythm of the piece and imposes real voyeurism on the audience.

Their response is no longer to the play or film but to the real, or simulated, actions of those taking part. As Robinson put it: "A work whose sexual content is left deliberately uncontrolled by the artist is pornographic—and is necessarily pornographic because the expression—the understanding of the audience—cannot be controlled as part of the work".

I think this is a pretty good definition of pornography, but it has, I think, some curious consequences. For instance, it makes nonsense of the view—usually advanced by half-witted actresses —that nude love making is permissible when the artistic integrity of the script demands it. (We had one of these dotty ladies in *Council of Love*. Having advanced every dishonest argument we could think of to persuade the cast of this piece to take their clothes off, we were informed, via a remarkably earnest Equity Official, who was a bit ginger, if you ask me, that Miss X, having pondered long and hard on the subject of artistic integrity, had decided that she could after all appear topless, but that she would expect to be rewarded to the tune of ten pounds a week extra. Five pounds a tit).

It follows, then, from Robinson's argument that nude love making is particularly to be avoided in a work of artistic quality, since it is precisely in such a context that the shock of being turned into a real voyeur will have the most destructive consequences. On the other hand, nude love making is to be encouraged in works whose sole intention is to turn the audience into voyeurs, and obligatory in those which are so lamentable that any inappropriate note is to be applauded.

It must be admitted, therefore, that the nude scene in *Hair* was an artistic mistake, since for the few moments it lasted one inevitably failed to have the intended response, but was assailed instead by such irrelevant thoughts as: "I wonder if they're cold", and "Goodness me, that fellow hasn't got a thing; oh no, it's Marsha Hunt".

The nudity in *Oh Calcutta* on the other hand, is necessary, since the audience are willing parties to a conspiracy whereby they will, for the duration of the piece, become real voyeurs and little else. And we can conclude that total nudity should be obligatory throughout such programmes as *Colditz, Special Branch, Up Sunday, Face the Music, Call my Bluff, My wife next door, Dave (smirk smirk I'm only joking) Allen at Large,*

What the Papers say, Michael Parkinson talks to Kenneth Williams, and, of course, *Rossel Harty Plos*, on the grounds that any response, however inappropriate, must be preferable to the one intended. (In fact, one should be more sympathetic, I think, towards the boot-lacking Parkarson and Rossel Harty Plus—even towards Parkarson on such blush-making occasions as his guest happens to be the boastful Harold Evans, in full slap, tripping down the staircase to the strains of "There's no business like showbusiness", while the salivering Parkarson waits to congratulate him on his breathtaking courage in putting in a word or two on behalf of the thalidomide children. Why Rossel Harty Plus and Parkarson are allowed to watch television, never mind appear on it, had been the mystery, but having seen Lindsay Anderson interviewing Rudolph Nureyev, I now think that they're not so bad after all.

L.A. Tell me, do you get nervous before one of your performances?

R.N. (After a long pause. He is scarcely able to believe his ears). Yes.

L.A. (Having considered the implications of this astounding answer). Yes. It's our destiny.

This explains why artists in general, and Lindsay Anderson in particular, so often appear to be cross. An artist would certainly not wish to have his destiny discussed in the idiom of a *Spectator* essayist. It's bewildering, though, when a person as talented as Lindsay Anderson makes such a prat of himself. It's dangerous too, since it's a background of such incidents that causes the quite irrational feelings of irritation that well up inside one when Lord Olivier, say, puts on his winter combinations and demonstrates on behalf of some ballet dancer who is not permitted to leave Russia.

Anyway, I said all this to Mrs. Raeburn, but very fast and just the wrong side of audibility, as a precaution against being contradicted. This being so, it wasn't surprising perhaps that when I eventually stopped, she said, quite distinctly: "I think Lord Longford is a very dangerous man". Not only had I never seen Long Longford in these terms, I couldn't see how this observation followed from what I'd been saying. When I challenged Mrs. Raeburn on this point, she said she'd taken my remarks (or such of them as she'd been able to hear) as some sort of attack on pornography. This had led her to mention Lord Longford, whom she once again referred to as a dangerous fellow. I must admit it quite surprised me to hear him spoken of in this way. Since I've always taken it as axiomatic that the truth should never be allowed to stand in the way of a huge, life-enhancing joke, I have always assumed the Lord L's activities were to be encouraged, if not actually subsidised by the Ministry of the Environment. True, his masochistic desire for public humiliation does turn the stomach from time to time, but most great clowns have their unfortunate side. On the whole, they perform a useful, even cathartic, function. Like streakers the most successful buffoons—Lord Hailsham, Enoch Powell, Sir Lew Grade, Mary Whitehouse, Brian Clough, Robin Day, Slipper of the Yard—unselfishly act out our secret fears in public, and in the process add a bit of salt and pepper to an otherwise tasteless stew. Sometimes they go too far in their efforts to shock (Lord Soper's recent observation on TV that "the trouble with young people is that they seem to think sex is normal" is an example of this), and then of course puritans like Anna Raeburn take offence. But on the whole I don't think their contributions to the debate are unallowably obscene, least of all those of Lord Longford. His speciality, as far as I can see, is nothing more corrupting than a persistent attempt to draw an inference concerning moral behaviour from a premiss consisting of an aesthetic judgement. This, I said sternly to Anna Raeburn, was not Ian Robinson's position at all. He stays rigidly within the field of aesthetics, as can be seen from the representative quote: "Pornography doesn't cause depravity and corruption: it *is* depravity and corruption". In fact, the first of these propositions is a precise denial of Lord Longford's conclusion. Except that I cannot for the life of me make out whether Lord L is saying "pornography is pleasant, but harmful", or "unpleasant, but harmful". (early on in any debate between the permissives and the anti-permissives it becomes clear that no language exists by which either side can convey to the other what they mean by sexual desire; Lord L could no more describe his sexual appetites to me than he could describe the colour orange to a blind man), I take his argument to run as follows: "A photograph of a man and a woman making love is pornographic; all pornography gives rise to wicked behaviour; everything that gives rise to wicket behaviour should be banned; therefore all pornography should be banned". This argument is valid, but that doesn't get us very far, because so is the argument: "all bald men should be banned; Lord Longford is a bald man; therefore Lord Longford should be banned". While it isn't logically impossible for bad taste to lead to bad behaviour (since the statement "this pornographic photograph caused me to commit rape" isn't self-contradictory) such as inference isn't logically necessary or even empirically so. Lord L himself seems to recognise this and in an effort to give his argument some authority he insultingly introduces mumbo-jumbo in the form of metaphysics. Thus, if challenged, he would presumably say that pornography is wicked because God says so. This argument is unanswerable, since it is not intelligible, but it could be pointed out that theologians have always agreed that Goodness and God's decrees are logically independent of one another. In the realm of empirical fact, there is little or no evidence that attendance at a blue film party is any more likely to give rise to depraved behaviour than attendance at the House of Lords. On the contrary, there is some evidence that the reverse might be the case, and should this evidence ever become overwhelming, then of course pornography ought to be made compulsory.

Mrs. Raeburn was jolly patient throughout all this, even though it didn't seem to have much to do with her group sex thesis. She did, however, give it as her opinion that my argument was becoming a trifle confused, and she asked me whether I was, on the whole, for or against pornography. I said that I thought this an absurd question, as absurd as to ask whether one was, on the whole, for or against sex. Because one was in favour of sex, this did not mean that one was necessarily in favour of sex with Lord Longford. Equally, an opinion that every blue film one had ever seen was disgusting did not mean that one would necessarily find disgusting a blue film featuring artistes who were more aesthetically pleasing than is the norm in this medium. All a question of aesthetics, I said; a point that liberal interventionists like the well-meaning people running *Forum,* just as much as Lord Longford, seemed to overlook. That most hard core porn *is* displeasing is not an opinion they would readily offer, since to do so would seem to them in some way to be acting repressively. Equally absurd is their much touted slogan that there are no rules in sex so long as there is mutual pleasure. Apart from the fact that this is itself a rule that might cause the mutual pleasure seekers to feel guilt, or at least anxiety, if pleasure for one reason or another was temporarily absent, its absurdity can be demonstrated by applying it to any other human past-time. Would it be sensible to say that anything is alright in football so long as both sides are enjoying themselves? What happens if all twenty-two players suddenly decide they would rather pick the ball up and run about with it? They did once, and the game wasn't banned : it was called something else. (Perhaps this is the answer to Lord Longford. Perhaps if I stop calling what I do "sex", I will cease to tread on his toes. In future I will call it "goodkindmanning". The conventions of goodkindmanning will fail to offend him, since they will by definition have nothing to do with the conventions of Christian sex). And—to return to the football analogy —would it be sensible to say that the game is only permissible if *all* the players are enjoying themselves? Manchester United certainly look as miserable as hell at the moment, but nobody has suggested that they be banned from playing. And if it is pointed out that football is a spectator sport, so frequently is goodkindmanning. I can see no harm in a wife's undressing in a particular way to please her husband, even though she herself gets no satisfaction from the ritual; and it is certainly arguable that the nude ballet in *Oh Calcutta* was beautiful and worthwhile, even though the two performers were probably not enjoying themselves, but on the contrary were miles away, fretting over their income tax returns or worrying whether they'd turned off the gas before coming to the theatre.

I'd run myself dizzy by this point, Ann Raeburn's eyes were beginning to glaze over, and it came as no surprise when she excused herself and left. I'm jolly grateful to her though. She has made me think about pornography and by doing so she has given me this alternative idea for an occupation. Rather than waste the expensive tape recorder that Emma Jane has at last bought me (after a great deal of far from subtle prompting on my part), I shall thrust its microphone under the noses of various pornographers and quiz them fearlessly as to their intentions. This should be just as much fun as the silly old police book, and almost as good a cover. "Living on artistic earnings? Bless my soul no! I'm a serious investigative reporter and if my researches require that I live in a brothel, then live in a brothel I must". Two years for poncing and two for answering back.

*　　*　　*

For some time now, Dawn Upstairs has been trying to persuade me to meet her important show business friend, the impresiario Toby Danvers. I have always pointed out that there is not a reason in the world why I should want to meet anyone from the world of entertainment (or from ATV either, for that matter), but she never listens to what I say, so to get it over with I agreed to meet him yesterday. The date was arranged for four o'clock at her flat: a choice of venue, which, though convenient, surprised me. I assumed for some reason that Danvers was a punter and I though it strange that he would be happy to discuss business in a setting likely to bring to mind, perhaps embarrassingly, frequent less formal rendezvous. Then it occurred to me that his willingness to meet here must spring, as did my own, from a guilt-free conscience. Now that I've met him, I realise how wide of the mark this second supposition was. Danvers is indeed a punter (when funds allow, which isn't always) and the notion that he might suffer guilt in this respect is laughable. The live theatre, after all, attracts some very peculiar fish indeed, remarkably few of them, alas, to be found on the working side of the footlights. Artistes, as they like to be called, tend to be disconcertingly humdrum, not over-endowed upstairs, as it happens, but cunning and hard as nails in business, and with a tendency to comfort themselves out of hours like elderly Edinburgh solicitors. The business men, on the other hand, are frequently saddled with imperfectly expressed artistic temperaments and are often, in consequence, as mad as hatters. Toby Danvers, I have now discovered, is one of the more attractively dotty of these entrepreneurs.

"He's bound to be a little late", said Dawn Upstairs, who was carrying on in a way I'd never seen before, nor imagined possible from such a delightfully unofficial person. Straight-backed upon a dainty chair, stiletto legs gracefully crossed, face set, an air of concentration as though threading a needle; this, she conveyed, was to be no laughing matter. Like most busy and successful people, Dawn Upstairs suffers from a super-abundance of energy and is naturally a fidget; but on this occasion she had recalled her early training at the Ballet Rambert and had somehow managed to compose her limbs into an artificial elegance of movement, so that all her gestures were elaborately slow and seemed to come from the centre and be completed, like a dancer miming. The effect was idiotic, and though I took it that Mr. Danvers must be a very big cheese indeed, I was sorry to see Dawn Upstairs go to pieces so completely. I had always supposed that her personality entirely lacked the formal side that we customarily display to those people—close relatives, hotel receptionists, bank managers, head waiters—whom we are trying to convince of our probity. How one is occasionally let down even by the people one most admires.

I was quite happy, however, to wait for such a busy man, even in this forbidding atmosphere. As it seemed likely that any attempt to communicate with Dawn Upstairs would, in her present mood, hit fog, I sat back patiently and gazed around the room. Being geared to turnover rather than comfort, tart's quarters often have the cold, unlived in aspect of hotel suites, but Dawn Upstairs's flat is surprisingly cosy, offering no clue as to how its occupant makes ends meet. Possible the bedroom is accoutred with all the time honoured aids to pleasure, but the room in which we sat didn't seem an appropriate setting for anything more depraved than the little tea-party now in progress. To a suspicious mind, it's true, the number of mirrors might have seemed excessive, and an eagle eye could possibly have twigged that the sofa on which we sat was extendable into a bed the size of a wrestling mat; but on the whole the furniture and decor could have been the choice of any conventionally switched-on lady, drawing a living in that vague no-man's land where models, actresses, boutique sales girls and air hostesses mingle and lose their special definition. Nor did the literature on view seem likely to inflame: *Vogue, Nova, Theatre World* (brought out perhaps for Mr. Danvers) and Anthony Sampson's *A New Anatomy of Britain* (possibly a handy directory of clients) lay casually upon a coffee table. The only distressing feature was a huge, almost life size photograph of Dawn Upstairs herself, taken, I'd say, ten years previously and showing her to be beautiful and carefree. I imagine she consults this frequently for reassurance, rather as an ineffectual man might study a portrait of some celebrated ancestor in search of a virtue he might have inherited.

When Toby Danvers at last arrived, he was so entirely different from the person I'd been expecting that I may have gaped at him a trifle rudely. The extraordinary behaviour of Dawn Upstairs had led me to imagine a clean, alert, spot-on young hustler with shrewd eyes and a suspiciously candid hand-shake. Instead, a jolly, shaggy Tweedledum of a man came rolling through the door, chortling and wheezing merrily, but seeming to walk with the difficulty of a man on the deck of a storm tossed ship. In fact he crossed the room carefully and in stages, pausing at intervals to steady himself on bits of furniture, as though the floor were moving beneath his feet. The initial impression he gave of considerable portliness was conveyed, I came to see, entirely by his head, which on closer inspection could be seen to be rather too big for the rest of him. His cheeks were pink and chubby and the knot of his tie was almost hidden from view under the folds of a heavy double chin, yet the overall impression was of a once very fat man who'd lost a lot of weight. His suit, which was of a traditional and expensive cut, had clearly seen better days and seemed to have been built for an older and stouter person. He wore a waistcoat which was as asymmetrically buttoned and he appeared not to have shaved. He greeted us cheerily, hugged Dawn Upstairs, roared with laughter when she offered him tea, negotiated with some difficulty the short distance to the drink tray, poured himself a devastating whiskey (some of it going in the glass), dropped the bottle, roared with laughter again and tottered towards the sofa with the exaggerated, jerky gait of a young rep actor forced by circumstances to play the part of a senile old gentleman.

"Well, well", he said, as he lowered himself carefully into a sitting position, "upon my word, this *is* pleasant".

He lay back, closed his eyes and fell instantly asleep. I liked him immensely and resolved that when he came round, we should do business together. It did seem possible, however, that this would not be the day to get the partnership off the ground.

"He's had a lot of worries recently, has Toby", said Dawn Upstairs, feeling, I suppose, that some form of explanation was called for.

"Poor soul".

"*Shit*".

"What?"

"*Shit*. The musical. He put it on, did Toby.

"My goodness. He must be doing well then".

"Oh he is. But he tires himself out. Too much on his plate".

"Too much on his plate, eh?"

"Yes. And his personal life is at sixes and sevens. He can't seem to settle down. He keeps falling in love with his secretary. Last week he threw the typewriter at her. Fortunately she ducked and it flew harmlessly out of the window into Dean Street".

"What are those red marks on either side of his forehead?"

"He's been having electric shock treatment. That's where they attach the wires".

"Will he wake up?"

"Not for an hour or two. He'll be quite all right after a little nap. Then I'll get him home".

She showed me to the door and apologised once again for the fact that the meeting had not been satisfactory. "Perhaps you could meet another time", she said.

"I'd love to. I like the look of him enormously. I do hope he gets his personal life sorted out. It's such a trial when that goes wrong".

"I suppose it is", said Dawn Upstairs, rather wistfully I thought. Perhaps Carwash Candy was giving her a hard time, or perhaps she was merely acknowledging that a life devoted to public service had never allowed her to put personal pleasures first.

So I returned to the flat without having achieved very much from my first meeting with Mr. Danvers. But I liked the cut of his jib enormously. I'm an excellent judge of character, and unless I'm much mistaken, here is a man who could make a most suitable business associate. I feel I'll be seeing more of him, and that at least is my intention.

*　　*　　*

Lunch with Tom Parkinson. Met him in his office up-west. He claims to be a film producer and I have no reason to disbelieve him. He is now able, when talking to agents down the phone, to refer to quite celebrated artistes by their surnames only. "I can get Curtis, but Sutherland's too expensive, etc., etc." This is one of the first things you have to be able to do. It's a bit of a comedown when you think that he used to be an Albert. I see hope for him, however. In the course of discussing some contract or other, he was okay till he had to say "force majeure", then he got the giggles. The fantasy began to slip, showing the amusing person underneath. To be a producer you have to be able to say things like "force majeure" and "above the line costs" without starting to laugh. Happily, I don't think this will ever be the case with Parkinson.

It was raining after lunch, so I took a taxi home, even though I had no money on me. I was assuming that Emma Jane would be in, and able to discharge my debt. Having let myself into the flat, I was a bit dismayed, therefore, to see no sign of her. Remembering that she sometimes leaves money in handbags not currently in use, I went into the bedroom and was much relieved to find her in bed with a man I'd not previously met. I knew he wasn't a punter, because had he been, certain security precautions, such as locked doors, would have been in force; but even so, I felt a bit of a fool barging in like that. Nor did I put them much at ease with my abrupt request for the loan of 50p. Emma Jane seemed quite confused, but her friend obligingly climbed out of bed and fished a pound note out of his trouser pocket. He really seemed a very decent fellow. I said I was most grateful and tried to convey by the geniality of my tone that he musn't feel bound to leave.

Having paid off the taxi driver, I pottered about Sloane Avenue for a while, not wanting to return to the flat until they'd had time to sort themselves out a bit. I couldn't have been gone for more than ten minutes, but when I returned upstairs, Emma Jane's new friend had left. I congratulated her on this marked improvement in her behaviour, but she didn't seem that pleased with herself.

"What an odd man", she said, "they're so difficult to get rid of these Australians, they're so insensitive".

I said that I'd thought he'd sounded American.

"Yes, he puts that on at first. Then he forgets and the Australian cuts through. It's like with Big Elaine. He's okay though, I suppose".

I asked what he did for a living, an irritating conversational tic of mine.

"Actually, he said he was a film producer, but his story kept changing. You know how these Australians are. They're all shop lifters really and they get confused".

This is true. Australia must be the only country in the world where the entire male population are criminals, and all the women molls. Furthermore, there is no stultifying system of specialisation, such as inhibits professionals in other countries. In England, say, you are a bank robber, or a fraudsman, or a peterman, or a solo creeper. In Australia this is not the case. The man who rigs the stock market also steals your colour television set while you're upstairs counting your jewellery; the financier who invites members of the public to buy shares in a non-existent marmalade mine, snatches old ladies handbags on the way to his colour supplement offices.

I asked Emma Jane where she'd met him.

"Outside the supermarket opposite. He hopped out of a car and did that tired bit about pretending to know me. Surely I was the well-known rhubarb, rhubarb, rhubarb, all that old-time stuff. At first he said he was a photographer. After a while he promoted himself to film director and finally he became a producer. I thought it was all fairly funny, so I played along. What do you think?"

"Any name?"

"Well, he was a bit confused about that too. At first he was Dick something, but when I called him that, he didn't answer. So I asked him again and he'd become Jim. I think he finally settled on Pete".

He looked like fun to me and I hope we see him again.

*   *   *

Emma Jane's 21st birthday. She insisted on celebrating the occasion with a small dinner out. The party was tremendous fun

and we all caught the clap. Not there and then of course; indeed
the disease has taken the customary day or two to manifest itself,
but it was an unforseen consequence of this get-together. We
were more or less the usual crowd, plus Farthingale. Farthingale
isn't really a friend, but since he was paying, we had to let him
eat with us. He is one of a small army of attentive, slightly ga-ga
young men, whom business girls refer to as their tin soldiers. (The
class of all mugs subdivides into the class of gonks and the class
of tin soldiers, and the two are not to be confused.) Their duties
are light. They run errands, help with the shopping, drive the
girls from one appointment to the next and come to the rescue
on occasions such as this. They're treated poorly on the whole
and what benefit accrues to them in return for the modest tax
the girls levy on their company it's hard to say. Marvellously
democratic as a rule in sharing out their favours, business girls
exclude tin soldiers, as a class, from the general distribution. This
parismony, they feel, keeps the tin soldiers on their toes. I don't
think a tin soldier ever graduates to the rank of gonk, but I
might be wrong. Certainly business girls avoid this circumstance
if they can; gonks are two a penny, but a good tin soldier is hard
to find. Farthingale, whose I.Q. must be in single figures, is currently the most mesmerised of these young men, and though too
dim to earn a living (he is even barred from the family firm), he
is yet in receipt of a weekly competence from Daddy which so
far hasn't buckled under the strain of Emma Jane's small demands. I wasn't too happy that this duffer should foot the bill
at our celebrations, but Emma Jane was adamant that the evening should be down to him.

Apart from Farthingale, the party consisted of a few of our
better friends: Motor Show Polly, back in London, after a
profitable year in the Lebanon; my friend S. Z. Corbett, Motor
Show Polly's current escort and therefore acceptable again
(Polly favours pretty black boys, whom she wears like matching
accessories and switches with dazzling frequency—trading up
she calls it); Twigg the well-known playwright, not much liked by
the rest of us, since he's illiterate and we suspect him of unnatural tendencies; Black Dolores, home again after her period
of meditation in India, and seemingly none the worse for it;
Dawn Upstairs with Carwash Candy; and Foxy Francis with
his latest secretary. Unusually attracted to temporary secretaries

with fat legs, Foxy is father confessor to the firm and known accordingly as the Bishop of Belgravia. A struck-off solicitor, to whom it was pointed out at the time of his lapse that in fastidious legal circles it was customary for officers of the court to advise their clients after they had committed a felony rather than before, the Bishop now runs a business efficiency school, which is rumoured to be going bust. Just before the kick-off, Dawn Upstairs rang to ask whether she might also bring my new friend Toby Danvers, the impresario, who had just turned up in her flat and showed no immediate sign of continuing on his way. I was delighted by this.

Farthingale arrived first, mumbling goofily and handing me an enormous bunch of roses. These, It transpired, were meant for Emma Jane, who was still in the bedroom getting dressed. Having thanked him politely on her behalf, I found myself stumped for further conversation was was most relieved when our other guests arrived in quick succession. First through the door were Dawn Upstairs, Carwash Candy (wearing a monocle) and Danvers the Impresario. Danvers seemed to be in rather better shape than at our previous meeting and was carrying an important looking briefcase, which had *Shit* stickers pasted to the outside. Once again, however, he seemed to doze off the moment he sat down.

Next to arrive were the Bishop and his secretary followed by Black Dolores, apparently walking in her sleep, and Twigg the well-known playwright, handing round copies of his recently published works, and looking, in leather, rather mutton dressed as lamb. The Bishop addressed his secretary as "my child" and introduced her, without embarrassment, as Miss Gloria Goodbody. He'd given, he said, his solemn promise to her father, a tax official in Bristol, that he'd keep an eye on her in London. Dawn Upstairs gave her a quick, professional looking over, like a burglar assessing the possibilities of a safe he might decide to crack, and then lost interest. I must say I agreed with her. Miss Goodbody didn't strike me as being altogether up to scratch, but Twigg the well-known playwright started patting his hair and talking to her out of the side of his mouth—always a sign that he is sexually aroused. She seemed to me to be lacking in conventional prettiness and her layers of puppy fat, inadequately covered by an absurd mini-skirt (like Nigel the Schoolmaster, now of British Intelligence, the Bishop does his shopping in the children's department of Marks and Spencer), made one fear that the old sod might be taking undue risks. The Bishop usually has better taste, but Twigg's interest was to be expected. He's none too choosey, to tell the truth, and his habitual randiness tends to make him something of a laughing stock. Business girls can't abide randy men and it's odd that he's been given a position on the firm. I think his function must be to make the rest of us feel superior. As Nietzche used to say : "Sometimes we owe a friend to the lucky circumstance that he gives us no cause for envy". Something like that.

Last to arrive were Motor Show Polly and S. Z. Corbett. Motor Show Polly is a big girl and always dresses with flair. On this occasion she'd come as a barrage balloon temporarily free of its moorings, or such was the first impression. Once one's eyes had adjusted to the glare, it could be seen that she was in a voluminous trouser suit of some fluorescent silver material. She looked magnificent, but it is generally felt that in S. Z. Corbett she may have met her match. Tonight he was at his most resplendent in British Racing Green, and his remarkable collection of jewellery sparkled about his person like decorations on a Christmas tree. Motor Show Polly, who's got a marvellous sense of humour, made a bee-line for Dawn Upstairs and greeted her in a fashion that some people might have found unorthodox. Carwash Candy assumed a menacing expression, and the Bishop, who's knocked around the world a bit and become in the process rather coarse, remarked :

'Upon my soul, thirty years ago such an incident would have given me an erection. Now, alas, it takes rather more than that".

His secretary recrossed her chubby legs and looked obscurely guilty. Twigg the well-known playwright patted his hair, and Farthingale, who'd been standing around awkwardly until this moment, now contracted a sudden infirmity of the legs, causing them to give beneath him, so that he sat down abruptly and impaled himself on the bunch of roses, which Emma Jane had thoughtlessly left lying on a chair. With a single profound oath, he rose from the chair like a leaping salmon and started to hop around the room, batting at his tortured backside like a man whose coat-tails are on fire. Blind with pain, no doubt, he tripped over Black Dolores, who was lying on the floor, struck a table and started bearing down on Danvers The Impresario, who, being sound asleep, was unable to avoid this unexpected ricochet, and was knocked backwards off his chair. People react unreliably when woken violently from their slumbers, but Toby Danvers's behaviour surprised us all. Screaming "help! help!" he hurled himself upon Farthingale, gripped him by the throat and began to shake him like a rat. Hypnotised by this unexpected turn of events, we all remained rooted to the spot, with the exception of Carwash Candy, who had the presence of mind to hit my new friend Danvers very hard over the head with a rolled up copy of *Penthouse*. The surprise of this assault from an unexpected quarter caused Danvers to losen his grip on Farthingale, who dropped backwards into an untidy heap, like a marionette suddenly abandoned by his manipulator. At this point, Danvers appeared to recover complete consciousness and his demeanour changed abruptly.

"Hullo", he said, smiling round the room, "what's going on? Why's that fellow lying on the floor? Nothing amiss, I hope".

As for Farthingale, he now lapsed into an apparently catatonic state, the symptoms involving muscular rigidity and mental stupor, alternating with a sudden, spasmodic jerking of the head in a clockwise direction. After about half an hour, however, he was in good enough shape to drive us to Tito's in his Daddy's Rolls. One could only hope that his cheque writing arm had in no way been impaired.

Tito's—one of those hopeful terrazzas that must have instilled in many people a life-long determination never to visit Italy—was the choice of Twigg the well-known playwright, who likes to dine among the latest faces. A general inclination not to sit next to Farthingale and specific requests from both the Bishop and Twigg that they should be allowed to sit with their back to the wall facing the door, caused the seating arrangements to be more than usually intractable to settlement. Twigg gave no reason for his preference (it was to enable him to leer at the modish as they entered), but the Bishop explained it was a habit he'd adopted since being assaulted from the rear by a Falangist in a Barcelona brothel.

"More likely you want to be able to spot your creditors coming in before they spot you", said Dawn Upstairs, with quite uncharacteristic sharpness. She and the Bishop are, as it happens, on rather prickly terms. It offends her business instinct, Pretty Marie once observed, that such a venerable old party has never become a punter.

The dinner proceeded normally, with the Bishop doing all the talking, Twigg the well-known playwright trying to pull Gloria Goodbody by offering her a part in his latest play (a desperate ploy of his), Black Dolores and my new friend Toby Danvers snoozing peacefully at opposite ends of the table, until Farthingale, as though to prove that his first success in the field of slapstick humour had been more than beginners' luck, suddenly set out on a conversation with Black Dolores, which, proceeding as it did on different levels and in opposite directions, was destined to land him up a cul-de-sac.

"Do you smoke, man?" he suddenly asked. The last word was no doubt well intentioned—an attempt to put her at her ease by a shot at what he took to be her idiom—but the word would have come unsuitably from him, even if his diagnosis of her gender had been more accurate.

Black Dolores, who'd been miles away, eyes closed, head nodding to private rhythms, with an effort focused blearily on Farthingale.

"Sure", she muttered, "when it's cool".

Farthingale looked momentarily baffled.

"Would you like one now?" he asked.

"Here?" said Black Dolores, her eyes opening a fraction wider in surprise, "wow, what a great idea". She started to reach across the table with a trembling hand, when apprehension gathered in her fuddled mind, and she turned to Dawn Upstairs for reassurance. "Darling", she said, her voice seeming to gather strength with hope, "is it cool to have a smoke?"

"*Here*?" said Dawn Upstairs, who hadn't heard the first part of the conversation, "Christ no, they'd throw us out. *Do* behave yourself".

"Sorry", said Black Dolores, turning back to Farthingale with a shaky smile of regret, "it seems they'd throw us out". She closed her eyes and started humming gently to herself.

Farthingale looked aghast and hastily stubbed out the cigarette he'd only recently lit.

"Good Lord", he said, thinking he was guilty of some colossal social gaffe, "I *am* sorry".

He went scarlet and, to cover his embarrassment, started to tip backwards and forwards in his chair. Inevitably one of the backward swings caught a passing waiter in the crutch, causing him to drop a plate of bolognaise and clutch his parts, a wordless, maniacal moan escaping from his lips. With a distraught cry, Farthingale leapt to his feet, skidded in the bolognaise and performed a kind of sliding football tackle on another passing waiter, causing him to drop a tray of coffee into the lap of my new friend Toby Danvers. Rudely shaken out of his slumber for the second time in the evening, Danvers on this occasion went instinctively into a kind of boxer's crouch and, snarling angrily, looked to right and left like a maddened bull trying to locate his assailant. Deciding, it seemed, that the waiter who'd been caught in the crutch was the most likely culprit, he put his head down and charged in that direction. Carwash Candy, alert now to this sort of situation, quickly put herself between Danvers and the waiter, thinking, I suppose, that she might somehow divert the charge or be able to step out of the way in the nick of time. Alas, she had underestimated the speed at which Danvers was covering the ground and, taking the full force of his weight somewhere around the navel, was laid out cold.

She got off the ground eventually, but the evening sagged a bit, until the surprise appearance in the restaurant of Emma Jane's Australian friend of the day before, accompanied by a rather po-faced model girl. Having first checked on who was picking up the jack and jill—as he put it—they joined our table. He turned out to be called Ken Pardoe (Emma Jane had got his name entirely wrong, unless he'd changed it in the last twenty-four hours, which, for an Australian, is perfectly possible of course) and the initial impression I'd received that he was most agreeable was quickly confirmed. He has an attractive, somewhat piratical face, with a crooked nose and eyes that are mischievous rather than predatory. His companion, on the other hand, made a less favourable impact. Stiff as a frozen fish, she seemed to be a throwback to the days when top models were required to stare chillingly at the camera as though it were a cigar impertinently lit before the loyal toast; and she reacted to all attempts to unbend her with the haughty forbearance of a premier danseur noble compelled by circumstance to appear in an Emile Littler panto. Perhaps she was shy. Her name, Baba (she seemed to have only the one) struck me as being about as daft as the rest of her. After a bit of discreet probing, I discovered that Ken's profession is to play the horses by day and five card stud at night, so when he suggested that we open a model agency together, I agreed.

"We'll only have top draw molls", he said, "like at Lucy Clayton's".

That made sense, but then he said that Baba would be our first client. I didn't much care for the sound of that (and nor did Baba, whose nostrils flared disdainfully at the news), but by the time the Bishop passed out over coffee, we'd arrived at a basic understanding. The Bishop was taken home by Gloria Goodbody and the rest of us went back to our flat. We had a smoke and after a while Baba the top model unexpectedly took off all her clothes and danced round the room with a silly expression on her face. No one had been paying her much attention up till them, but even so this solution seemed inappropriate. Like all model girls she had looked better in her clothes, being, as my new friend Ken the Australian horse player would say, a bit skinny in the old Dutch pegs. Her thighs failed to meet at the top, which is very unbecoming, I think, and her bottom was flat like a fellow's. The situation was unpromising, I thought, so I went to bed.

When I woke up in the morning, everyone had gone except Toby Danvers The Impresario. He was asleep on the sofa, fully clothed, with one arm draped protectively round his briefcase with the *Shit* stickers. We were most careful not to bring actual bodily harm upon ourselves by waking him.

*   *   *

All this was a few days ago and now there is this ridiculous business with the clap to contend with. How, I would like to know, did we all catch it that night, and who brought it among us? My money, not that I have any, is on Baba the top model. If that was her normal form, heavens knows what compromising situations she'd danced herself into recently. But how in one short night did she distribute it round ten self-respecting people,

117

one of whom at least had been asleep? Challenged on this point, Emma Jane has admitted nothing other than that during a lull she locked Baba the top model in the bathroom with Farthingale (as a consolation, she said, for the miserable evening he'd had), but one doesn't need a computer to calculate that the matter could hardly have stopped there.

Still, in a situation such as this, it is profitless to speculate, still less to cast aspersions; better to get the whole thing cleared up as quickly as possible. Accordingly, all those afflicted or under suspicion mustered in our flat at six o'clock this evening with the intentions of driving to Paddington General for a communal check-up. Everyone was cheerful, with the exception of Twigg the well-known playwright, Baba the top model and Farthingale, and there seemed to exist in the room that nervous bonhomie traditionally found in circumstances of shared adversity— such as blackouts, summer holidays and formal dinner parties. Twigg looked absurdly vexed, Baba the top model had re-assumed her icy mask and the news of his misfortunte seemed to have hit Farthingale like a wrecking ball from outer space. He had come down in a chair like a ruined house and his naturally ruddy complexion had turned the colour of herring roe. Black Dolores didn't seem to have a particularly firm grip on what was happening, but everyone else was intent on establishing that this was his or her first attack. Everyone, that is, except Ken the Australian horse player, who cheerfully claimed that this was the eleventh occasion at least that he'd been "up before the stewards".

"There's nothing to it", he said, "one shot up the Khyber and the old eight day clock's as good as new".

Farthingale squeezed us all into his Daddy's Rolls and managed, in spite of his shocked condition, to drive us to the appropriate wing of Paddington General. Here we parted company with the ladies and joined a queue of suitably crestfallen looking men waiting to be treated. Ken the Australian horse player, whom I find myself liking more and more, did his best to cheer everyone up with a selection of humourous stories that might have seemed rather near the knuckle at a convention of Wagga-Wagga sheep dippers, but the conditions were working against him. It was indeed impossible not to feel obscurely guilty, as though one had done something wrong, and being allotted a number as one entered had unfortunate custodial associations. The treatment, however, didn't seem designed either to humiliate or cause undue pain, nor did the doctor display a particularly censorious attitude. It would be boring, I suppose, to read the riot act a hundred times a day.

We were treated and back in the Rolls a good half-hour before the ladies, for reasons that became apparent when they finally appeared. The delay, it seemed, had been caused by Motor Show Polly, who had hogged the doctor's attention for a good half hour. She certainly seemed to have had the time of her life, and on the way home she gave us a detailed account of her consultation, in the course of which I at last discovered some of the background to our present troubles.

"My goodness me", she said, "I'm afraid that poor little doctor may never be the same again. But he was rather naive, didn't you find? I felt that he had to be told. You know how they ask you who you've been to bed with recently, and then write all the names down in that rather sinister way? Well, I had to tell him the truth, didn't I? Let me see now", I said, "there's my girl friend's fiance"—he blinked a bit at that—"and my girl friend"—at that point he took off his spectacles and wiped them, as though to get a better look at me—"and *my* boyfriend, S. Z. Corbett, and Twigg the well-known playwright, and Farthingale, and a charming Australian gentlemen, whose name for the moment escapes me". "I am sorry", she said, turning to Ken the Australian horse player, "in the excitement of the moment, I quite forgot your name. Do forgive me".

"Think nothing of it", said Ken. "I often forget it myself".

Very likely, I thought.

"Anyway", continued Motor Show Polly, "he then asked me whether it would be difficult to get in touch with all these people. They must be informed, he said, of their condition. So I told him that they were all outside waiting to be treated. Do you know, he appeared to be totally thunderstruck by this? He put down his pen very carefully and stared at me. Then he got up and went outside to have a look.

"I see", he said at last, "so you all know each other then?"

"Naturally", I said.

He looked rather dazed, but pulled himself together sufficiently to give me that little lecture about not having sex or alcohol for a month. Well, I wasn't going to let him get away with it as easily as that, was I?

' What precisely", I said, "do you mean by sex?"

"Copulation", he said.

"I see", I said, "so presumably it would be alright for me to go to bed with my girlfriend, would it?"

"Er—perhaps", he said, with a strange look in his eye, "perhaps you had better tell me exactly what you and your girlfriend er—ah—eum—" My God, that man knew *nothing*. I had to tell him *everything*. I can't imagine what they teach them at medical school. Well, of course, by the time I'd finished he was absolutely fascinated, and now he wants to meet us all. He gets off at eight, and I rather stupidly said he could have dinner with us. I'm afraid he's probably a bit randy. Doctors often are in my experience. Isn't that odd? Anyway, he's quite sweet really, and I thought it might be useful to have a specialist on the books".

*　　*　　*

Toby Danvers the Impresario has come to live with us. No formal arrangements have been made, but each night he falls asleep on the sofa in what my new friend Ken the Australian horse player calls the loungeroom, and each morning he's still there. Since he is most stimulating company when awake, this state of affairs suits me excellently; but Emma Jane is beginning to look anxious. He has no money, so she now has two old parties to feed, and his apparently defective sense of spatial relations does cause a certain amount of damage to his immediate environment. So far he has smashed six glasses, spilt coffee and red wine on the carpet, set fire to one of the new Habitat armchairs and blown the door off the oven. He did this by turning the oven on, failing to light it before going to fetch a cigarette, and on his return lighting not the oven, but the grill. The explosion was considerable, and to add to the fun Big Elaine happened at the time to be receiving a punter, who, suspecting an I.R.A. ambush, ran bare-arsed into the corridor screaming "fucking Irish!"

I tell Emma Jane that all this is a small price to pay for the prestige that inevitably accrues to a girl who has not one ponce, but two. She isn't impressed by this argument and points out that she doesn't want one ponce, never mind two, and furthermore that if she did want a ponce he wouldn't be very much like me. By which she means to imply that I'm too decrepit for the job. Rubbish, I say, and I try to make her see how much more reassuring it is to come home after a hard day's work to a mellow old fruit like me than to a funky little blackguard, who'd slap her round the face and confiscate the takings.

All the relevant facts concerning Danvers's background are now in my possession, and I approve of everything I've heard. He's been up and down like a fiddler's bow, but as he's presented some twenty shows and only had six nervous breakdowns, he considers himself to be ahead. After his last serious crack-up, his analyst advised him to work for a spell within the comforting structure of a large organisation, and it was while presiding over the theatre division of such a conglomerate that he produced *Shit*. The spectacular success of this musical caused him to take its somewhat Marcusean message rather too literally, and shortly after it opened, he walked out of his office without apprising his fellow directors of his intentions and went to live with a tribe of hippies, who were squatting in a country house in Dorset. And had it not been for the incident of the electric kettle, he might still be there. Toby Danvers is a man of infinite goodwill, but he has a magisterial streak and he cannot abide liberty takers. When he discovered his electric kettle hidden in the kit-bag of one of the hippies, he took the offender by the ear and marched him, together with the kit-bag, to the local police station.

"I wish to charge this young scoundrel with the burglarisation of my electric kettle", he said to a surprised desk sergeant.

"Ho yes, where is it?"

"In the fellow's kit-bag".

"Let's have a look then", said the sergeant, and he tipped the contents of the kit-bag on to the floor. He picked up the electric kettle and put in on the desk. "You say this kettle is yours?"

"Certainly I do".

"I see. And you are alleging that this—er—young—er—what's it here intended to deprive you of it permanently?"

"That, my good man, is precisely what I'm alleging and it

would behove you to charge him and lock him away for the night".

The sergeant at this point took the lid off the kettle and looked inside.

"This kettle is definitely yours?"

"Of course its mine", said Mr. Danvers, becoming cross. "I said it was and I am not accustomed to having my word doubted. Get a grip on yourself my good man. Do you intend to charge the young shaver or not?"

"Hang on, hang on. Not so fast now, not so fast. There can be no possibility of a mistake? This *is* your kettle?"

"Without a shadow of doubt".

"In that case", said the sergeant, putting his hand into the kettle and producing half an ounce of hashish, "in that case, perhaps you might be so good as to explain what this here might be".

"That", said Mr. Danvers, "is, as a child of six could see, a piece of cooking chocolate. Thank you for drawing it to my attention". He took the lump of hash out of the sergeant's hand and swallowed it.

He was carried singing to his cell and shortly fell into a deep and blissful sleep. While he slept, the local authorities went through his pockets and established his identity. The Managing Director of the firm for which he worked, a snake-eyed opportunist who had once been a foot juggler's assistant, arrived on the scene within twenty-four hours and, taking advantage of Mr. Danvers carefree condition, stole his shares and induced him to resign his directorship.

Returning to London, Danvers decided that he'd reached an age when a gentleman must keep a weather eye open for old biddies who are no better than they should be and, more importantly, own the property in which they live. For the last year or so, a succession of these randy aunties has kept him more or less above starvation level, while he has plotted and schemed to, as he puts it, "get the show back on the road". In the meantime he had another, more serious, misunderstanding with the law. In association with a film producer, who had also hit a bad patch, he went for a period into the stolen cheque book business. The film producer looked like a creeper, as film producers so often do, so he did the actual creeping, while Danvers, who has never lost his stately and plausible front, went round the shops acquiring easily marketable goods. Being amateurs, it was not long before they found themselves standing shoulder to shoulder in court. The film producer went down, but Danvers, thanks to his superior breeding and impeccable mode of address, got off with a bollocking. At least he thinks he did. He may have got a suspended sentence into the bargain, he says, but he's none too sure. When I suggest that he looks into the matter, since it could have bearing on his future treatment at the hands of the judiciary, he says he's simply not interested. (I have found that this vagueness concerning their sentence often afflicts people after an appearance in court. Stella who Stutters and One-eyed Charlie, for instance, were recently up at the Old Bailey, following the raid on their premises by the Drugs Squad, and neither one of them has the slightest idea whether they were found guilty or innocent. This is not so surprising as it may seem. On the only occasion that I've attended a criminal trial, I was greatly struck by the fact that I couldn't hear a blind word being said, and nor, clearly, could anyone else. There was a lot of mumbling and coughing under wigs and a few wet legal jokes, but it would have been only too easy to miss the actual sentence. In such circumstances, a prisoner is hardly likely to ask the judge to repeat it; better to clear off as quickly as possible and hope for the best.)

When I say that Danvers has no money, this is not entirely true. A great deal of his time is devoted to an intriguing running battle with the welfare state. He is of the opinion that they should subsidise him each week to the tune of £13, but they take the view that this should not be an infinitely extendable arrangement. Each week they like to be convinced anew that he is a deserving case. The opening shot in these highly ritualised manouveres is what is known as the Monday run. This is the high spot of the week. Every Monday morning, Mrs. Armstrong, a gin soaked old biddy who happens to own a car, sets off on a tour of the neighbourhood, in the course of which she picks up at previously arranged vantage points a various collection of well-born scroungers, including Danvers, whom she conveys to the labour exchange. Here, a tremendous barney takes place, during which the welfare state suggests to Mr. Danvers that he should seek employment as a short order chef in a Wimpey bar or as a kitchen porter at the Strand Palace Hotel, which he reminds them that he is a person of some quality, the producer of "Shit" no less, and that it would behove the sharp-nosed lady interrogating him to keep a civil tongue in her head when addressing her betters. Within a few days of this confrontation, a giro cheque for thirteen pounds sometimes arrives and sometimes it doesn't, according, it seems, to the mood of the sharp-nosed lady. When it doesn't, Danvers becomes bug-eyed with indignation and when it does, he disappears for a nerve-racking forty-eight hours, during which we phone round the various nicks to discover which one is holding him on a D. & D. charge. He is invariably fined two pounds and he always asks for time to pay. On the last occasion the Beak asked him politely whether he was currently employed.

"Not at the moment, Me Lud", said Mr. Danvers at his grandest, "but I have various schemes".

It is generally agreed that he was jolly lucky not to get six months on the spot. He swears he's finished with the laughter and heartbreak of the live theatre, but I have my doubts. Each Thursday he smuggles a copy of the *Stage* into the flat, which I catch him reading rather wistfully. I fear that he dreams of having his revenge on the various lightweight sharks who he imagines have done him down.

Meanwhile, I have formed a convenient theory round which to hang my interviews with various pornographers. Most pornography, in so far as it is created and purveyed by men for the delectation of other men, would seem to be a reflection of male frustration, a recognition of some disparity between male and female needs. Since our culture requires women to be provocative and inhibited at one and the same time, this disparity, whether biologically inevitable or the result of centuries of conditioning, is bound to be considerable. (E. G. Jane Birkin's recent admission concerning her early taste for flashing: "It was showing off really, being wicked and yet completely safe. It's nice to give chaps a chance to admire your body without all that boring business of keeping them off the grass afterwards. Actually when it comes to the crunch, nobody is more cowardly than I am. Directly its off with the shoes and everything. I'm out of the front door in a flash".) Since this apparent asymmetry between male and female requirements clearly entails pornography (it could hardly be the other way round, though I suppose a woman might claim that it was the glimpse of a dirty picture at an impressionable age that had conditioned her into becoming demure), it follows that everyone who wishes to see an end to pornography (those who don't need do nothing) should work towards the abolition of this discrepancy between male and female needs. Since it is unthinkable that the male population of the country should undergo some form of mass aversion therapy, it follows that the female element in the community should be educated into behaving in reality as spontaneously as they customarily do in male fantasies, as reflected in pornography.

If this theory is coherent, it follows that hard core porn, being aesthetically unpleasing and therefore nearer to the reality of most people's sexual experience, is more honest and less likely to breed anxiety and envy than the fraudulent, peek-a-boo filth peddled by J. Walter Thompson and Hugh Hefner (and therefore, Lord Pokinghorn should note, much less of a threat to family life and the monogamic virtues).

Accordingly, I have divided the pornographers I wish to interview into four groups : the Goodies, the bad Goodies, the good Baddies and the bad Baddies.

For the class of Goodies, which includes every sort of whore, from the expensive call girl to "Fifi, young model third floor", I have nothing but praise and respect. Without state aid or official encouragement, they accept and neutralise the pent-up, surplus sexual energies of the entire community.

The class of bad Goodies, which includes night club hostesses, visiting masseuses, sauna bath manageresses and escort agency girls, fails to merit total approval since its members are more capricious. A perhaps-I-will, perhaps-I-won't element tends to creep into their arrangements, and there is always a danger that the punter will depart in a more dangerous condition vis-a-vis the community than that in which he arrived.

The class of good Baddies consists of all those variously employed in the field of hard core porn : blue film artistes, proprietors of dirty bookshops and participants in live sex shows. They tantalise rather than provide, but they're honest and cheerful, and their version of reality is more accessible to the average person than the deceitful gloss offered by the soft core entrepreneurs.

This last class, the bad Baddies, consists of people—proprietors of girlie magazines, fashion models, producers of exploitation pictures, actresses who disrobe when their artistic integrity demands it, editors of women's magazines such as *Cosmopolitan* and *She,* model schools like Lucy Clayton's, which specialise in training girls to become female impersonators—in whose version of reality the notion of desirable sex is seamlessly interwoven with material advancement and a high income. By advertising a fantasy world in which unnaturally flawless, totally passive women—provocatively naked, but palpably unattainable—become mere status objects for rising executives, they induce masturbatory day dreams of a most unsettling nature. Few would leave their wives for the mottled, varicose veined scrubbers falling about in blue films (most men, exposed to *Deep Throat,* would return forthwith to home and family), but the Manikin commercials, are, it seems to me, seriously upsetting. (In this respect, I include Tynan among the villains. Whether he succeeded or not, his intention in *Oh Calcutta* was to turn the audience on. At an early discussion I had with him and Peter Brook about his show, Brook declined to direct it on the grounds that the only point of an erotic entertainment would be to bring the audience to a climx; this, he said, would not be possible in a theatre, but if we cared to open a brothel, he would be interested in directing it. Tynan should have taken his advice, I think. To turn an audience on is irresponsible, it seems to me, unless facilities are made available backstage, whereby the maddened voyeurs can have their pleasure of those who have spent the last two hours winding them up.)

I shall try to talk mainly to those pornographers of whom I disapprove. Taking only one or two practitioners from the class of Goodies and the class of bad Goodies—one call girl, say, and one masseuse—and one or two from the class of good Baddies—a blue film artiste, perhaps, and a dirty bookshop proprietor—I shall concentrate on those who are beyond redemption. I have in mind such as: Lucy Clayton, Vic Lownes, Michael White, Simpson and Galton, Fiona Richmond, Bob Guccione, Ray Cooney, Susannah York, Jilly Cooper, the Chairman of J. Walter Thompson, Evelyn Laye, Rupert Murdoch and Barbara Hulanicki, whose latest Kenginston store contains, I gather, a Mistresses department, specialising in slinky lingerie. (Nobody with whom I've spoken finds the assumption that there are two sorts of women—wives, who are homely and reliable, and mistresses, who are sexy and perverse—either funny or alarming). Preliminary researches indicate that one interesting side issue will be to discover the extent of the quite heated disapproval that each class of pornographers feels for the others. Grand brasses, for instance, consider night club hostesses and strippers very down the market; strippers feel superior to whores; dear old Maisie La Touche, a top tart for many years, stormed in rage out of the offices of the leading model agency that suggested she pose for underwear advertisements; actresses who run naked through exploitation pictures think ill of the girls who model for *Men Only*; film stars are forever suing *Playboy* for publishing photographs they seem to forget they posed for in the first place, and all classes burn with a pure and perfect contempt for *The News of the World*.

* * *

We received a shock this morning, from which it may take days to recover. At about ten o'clock there was a ring on the front door bell. I was having my morning cup of coffee, Mr. Danvers was in the bath, and Emma Jane and Big Elaine were still asleep. I crept into the hall and peeped through the spy hole. The only person I could see was a rather nice looking woman, who might have been a social worker of some sort. Normally one wouldn't dream of opening the door to a stranger, but she was of an unmenacing aspect, so for once I did.

"Good morning", she said, "is Mrs. Mouse in?"

"Certainly not", I said, genuinely surprised, "she doesn't live here. Might I ask who you are?"

"Don't be alarmed", said the nice looking woman, "but I'm Detective Sergeant Salisbury. It's not a serious matter, but we would like to speak to her. Can you tell us where she is?"

God Almighty, I thought, what has my little wife done? It couldn't be non-payment of parking fines, because she doesn't drive. And how had they traced her to this address?

"She's in Spain", I said, "I happen to know that".

This was the truth, but I didn't expect Detective Sergeant Salisbury to believe me. Dangerous criminals are always in Spain when wanted by the police.

"I see", said Detective Sergeant Salisbury, "well, as I say, it's nothing to worry about, but if you see her, perhaps you could be so good as to get her to ring me. I'll write down my name and phone number for you".

She tore a piece of paper out of her notebook and wrote down the necessary particulars.

"This may make her think it's more serious than it really is", she said, handing me the piece of paper, "but do tell her it's nothing to worry about".

I took the piece of paper, on which was written "Detective Sergeant Salisbury—Serious Crimes Squad".

This alarmed me considerably, in spite of D/S Salisbury's reassuring words. Bert "The Old Grey Fox" Wickstead's heavy mob don't waste time on trivialities. What on earth had my little wife been up to? My curiosity got the better of my extreme reluctance to have any close dealings with the police.

"Well, that does look a little worrying", I said. "In fact I'm her husband. Perhaps you'd better come in and tell me what it's all about".

"Thank you very much", she said.

I showed her into the living room and offered her a cup of coffee. It was not until I was in the kitchen attending to this matter that the full significance of what I had done came home to me. Here was I, a self-evident ponce, receiving the Serious Crimes Squad in the inner sanctum of a brothel, while another ponce, for whose arrest there were enough warrants out to paper the ballroom at the Grosvenor House Hotel, was taking his morning ablutions, and while the ladies of the establishment slept off their exertions of the night before. If Big Elaine suddenly appeared, I realised, we were goners. One glimpse of her and Detective Sergeant Salisbury would surely summon a black maria and take us all to West End Central. Worse, I suddenly remembered that there were enough soft drugs on display in the living room to stone the entire United States army, to say nothing of a collection of erotica that would certainly seem excessive anywhere but in a bawdy house.

I returned to the living room, expecting to find D/S Salisbury arranging the evidence against us into neat piles, but she was in fact sitting calmly in a chair, staring at nothing in particular. She had put her notebook on the coffee table, some six inches from an ounce of pot neatly wrapped in silver paper, and she was using an ashtray that contained the butts of three joints. On the sofa lay a bull whip, which Big Elaine had recently acquired in the Portobello Road, and on one of the side tables was a set of pornographic photographs of Emma Jane, taken by British Intelligence.

"Why", I asked, trying to appear cool and no doubt failing, "do you wish to see my wife?"

"In fact", said D/S Salisbury, "it's to do with the Norma Levy business".

How an upright citizen would react to the news that the Serious Crimes Squad wished to speak with his little wife in connection with the Lambton scandal, only occurred to me some time after D/S Salisbury had left. First, he would be stunned into silence, then outrage would grip him, he would demand to be told the source of these scurrilous rumours and, when this was not forthcoming, he would stomp off to Scotland Yard to lodge a stiff complaint. I, on the other hand, overcome by the irony of a situation that involved the Serious Crimes Squad's stumbling into a vice den while searching for someone who had probably never heard of Norma Levy, let alone met her, began to laugh, and, when this initial hysteria had subsided, to embark, for reasons that now seem to be obscure, upon the story of my life. Born into a nouveau riche shipping family, I began, my early education had been entrusted to Winchester College, an academy of some standing of which D/S Salisbury might have heard. After a statutory period in the Navy, in the course of which I had become interested in classical ballet and embarked upon a rather odd correspondence with Richard Buckle, I had gone to Cambridge, where I had fallen under the spell of John Bird and Dr. Leavis. Bird had proved the more decisive influence and I had consequently spent the next fifteen years clinging like a *moule marinière* to the outer and least salubrious edges of show business. My interests now centred round football, pornography and, saving D/S Salisbury's presence, police corruption, and I was acquainted, tangentally, with Ned Sherrin and the Bishop of Southwark. Indeed I had once dined with the latter at the House of Lords, a jolly occasion, in the course of which Field Marshal Montgomery had stopped at our table to have a word with the Bishop, showing himself in the process to be absolutely bats. My previous convictions, I said, included one for contravening the Dangerous Drugs Act, but happily I was still at large, as D/S Salisbury could see for herself, whereas two of the arresting officers on that occasion were now in the pokey for perjury and conspiracy to pervert the course of justice.

In the meantime, I said, I was lunching this very day with my friend Scott the Screenwriter, whose latest film *Don't Look Now* had been well received by the critics, though I myself doubted the wisdom of including the nude love scene between Julie Christie and the other fellow, an opinion with which I hoped D/S Salisbury would feel free to disagree if so inclined.

I must say that D/S Salisbury didn't seem in the least interested in any of this and would, I think, have left at this point but for the unexpected appearance in the room of Mr. Danvers, stark naked from the bath. Danvers has none of the modesty that normally assails those who look better in their clothes and he advanced purposefully into the room. I thought it best to mark his card.

"This", I said, enunciating the words unnaturally, as though speaking to a foreigner, "is *Detective Sergeant Salisbury* of the *Serious* Crime Squad. May I introduce Mr. Aloysius Birtwhistle, the producer of *Shit*".

Why I took the precaution of giving him an alias, followed immediately by his correct professional qualifications, I don't know; but the peculiar nature of the introduction did have the effect of making him wary. Instead of saying "If you're the Serious Crime Squad, I'm Mad Frankie Fraser", or some such rubbish, he squinted hard at D/S Salisbury, then at me, then at D/S Salisbury again, and finally said:

"In that case, perhaps I will go and put my clothes on", implying that this was not a social convention he customarily observed, but one that he would nonetheless follow on this occasion out of deference to the constabulary.

D/S Salisbury was beginning to show symptoms of bewilderment, which the sudden appearance in the room of Big Elaine did little to disperse. How *she* made her living could not have been clearer had she been dressed in a black corset, brandishing the bull whip and handing round brochures with her professional qualifications printed in dayglow lettering. Once again I made the necessary introductions.

"Detective Sergeant Salisbury, this is Big Elaine".

"I'm zo pleesed to meet wiz you", said Big Elaine, using one of her foreign accents, since a stranger was present, "I'm in caterin' ".

"Detective Sergeant Salisbury wants to meet my wife".

"Ah, si, si, that is nice. A so sweet girl. You'll like 'ur velly much".

At this point D/S Salisbury seemed to decide that she had had enough, and she got up and made for the front door. As I showed her out, I expressed my surprise that the investigation into the Lambton business was still going on some months after the scandal had first broken. Furthermore, I said, the Old Grey Fox seemed to be casting his net in rather elaborate patterns if he considered my little wife, who had, without a doubt, been further from the centre of the affair than Cardinal Heenan and the Dowager Lady Birdwood, relevant to his enquiries. D/S Salisbury agreed that the authorities were being thorough and confirmed that they intended to speak with everyone whose name was put forward by a prankster.

"Do you mean", I asked, "that if I now gave you the name of a girl out of the blue, you'd go and visit her?"

"Certainly", said D/S Salisbury, "if you said she was a friend of Norma Levy's".

Resisting the temptation to blow the whistle on a certain person's wife, I ushered D/S Salisbury out and assured her that I would get Mrs. Mouse to ring her on her return from Spain.

Big Elaine, Emma Jane and Mr. Danvers are a trifle alarmed by the implications of this incident, but I take the view that D/S Salisbury will report back to her superiors that she walked by mistake into a mad house and that we should be left alone. The police, I know, hate to have dealings with lunatics, lest they be held responsible for their condition. Indeed, my friend Diamond Pat Clancy, with whom I ran a theatrical agency, always carried a bar of soap in his top pocket and more than once escaped from the hands of the law by biting on this so that he foamed at the mouth. While this embellishment was probably superfluous in his case, I take his thinking to be correct and I'm confident that we will hear no more of the Serious Crimes Squad. Meanwhile, we should take full advantage, it seems to me, of the prestige that will now inevitably accrue to us as the only people in our immediate circle to have received such a visit.

Emma Jane is worried about the drugs and erotica, which she feels D/S Salisbury must have noticed, but I take the view that the police only investigate one offence at a time. If the definition of rationality is an ability to make connections between unalike events, the fuzz seem to fail in this respect, apparently being unable to conjure with two ideas at once. If they came to arrest you for feeding a parking meter, they would, I believe, fail to take the dead boy on the floor, the prniting press churning out fivers in the corner and the bulging sacks marked swag as evidence of any additional criminal activity.

One unexpected sequel to this incident has been the total lack of interest evinced by my inartistic friends.

"Guess what", I say, "there was a ring on the bell this morning and half the Serious Crimes Squad fell through the door". Naturally I touch up the details somewhat.

"Fancy that", they say, "isn't the price of meat a scandal?"

I have become quite paranoid over this reaction, but I think my irritation stems from an error of my own. For obscure reasons, I continue to make the mistake of numbering myself among the class of respectable citizens. The self-image I retain is of a cheerful, reliable, eager to please, easily shocked, animal loving public schoolboy of about eighteen : inexperienced as yet in the ways of a wicked world, but likely to mature within a few years into the sort of clean-cut young man any ordinary mother would choose as the ideal dancing partner for her daughter at a junior hunt ball. My inartistic friends, for some reason, fail to see me in this light and their interest could never be aroused by the Serious Crimes Squad's calling on me : only by their failure to do so.

*　　*　　*

Lunch with .6 of a friend Bassett, who brought with him a very nice, noisy lady called Hilary Pritchard. I didn't know who she was and consequently drew attention to the fact that she talked like Joan Greenwood. It was pointed out to me that she was the sexy lady with the Donald Duck voice who had once enlivened that dreadful Braden Beat, and that this was the nine hundred and seventy-sixth time that the slight resemblance between her voice and Miss Greenwood's (to say nothing of Fenella Fielding's or Broderick Crawford's) had been remarked upon. A poorish start.

I spoke of my plans to talk with pornographers and of my solution to the Lord Longford problem. The fallacy, I explained, had consisted in using one word—sex—to describe two entirely dissimilar activities. Sex might be okay, I said, (I had no way of knowning, since I'd never experienced it) but I'd wager that goodkindmanning was even better. Miss Pritchard said that I was very behind the times and that love was now the thing. No man would go to bed with her, she said, without, at some stage of the proceedings, telling her that he loved her. That didn't mean very much, I said, since without a doubt only a man with a tendency to say such things would be granted the privilege of intimacy in the first place. I refrained from quoting Groddeck's observation (since it didn't occur to me to do so) that "I love you is said when hate or indifference is pressing forward. It is uttered to cover the first little promptings of dislike". How sad it must be, said Miss Pritchard, never to have experienced Romantic love. What a thing to say to me!

Good heavens, I said, I'd be the last to deny the existence of Romantic love. I merely contended that, in my experience, it had nothing to do with sex, or rather goodkindmanning.

Women, said Miss Pritchard, were nowadays as sexy as men. Ten times sexier, I said, and that was the trouble. Tending to be monogamous by inclination, they wanted only one man, whereas it took ten to satisfy them. Men, who can be satisfied, no annihilated, by one woman, want by a perverse irony of nature, ten at least. "Pshaw"! said Miss Pritchard, "you're an old fashioned pervert". That was as may be, I said, but if I was, I had been since the age of six. Lord Longford couldn't claim that I'd been corrupted by the permissive society. At dancing class I used to have smutty fantasies about the little girls. Lord

133

Longford might contend, however, that but for the permissive society I would have grown out of this infantile stage, and were he to do so, I'd agree with him as it happens.

When I got home, I realised that I should have asked Miss Pritchard how frequently she masturbates, since I fail to see how adherentst o the sex = emotional involvement school of thought accommodate this practice within their theory. Emma Jane, for instance, who is also of Miss Pritchard's way of thinking, masturbates five times a week at least. With whom is she emotionally involved at such moments? I ask myself. With Emma Jane there also arises the awkard (to her theory) question of her bisexuality. Her rigid selectivity, her conviction that emotional involvement is a condition of good sex, breaks down completely when it comes to other girls. If you told her that she had to go to bed with a man she's never met, she'd be scandalised and call the cops (I'm not speaking of her professional life, of course), but if you told her that Miss X the black go-go dancer from Le Club Plonk was coming round, she'd be all agog. She cheerfully admits that only a handful of men have ever satisfied her, whereas no girl has ever failed in this respect. And the great majority of bisexual girls make the same claim. Yet they are certainly not lesbians. The idea of a continuing relationship with another girl would seem to them quite grotesque. Emma Jane would agree, I think, with the point of view expressed by Germaine Greer when she said that "lesbian lovemaking is very good from the orgasm point of view, but ultimately boring". By 'boring' she presumably means 'lacking in significance', failing to fulfil the conditioned need for emotional reassurance. Better a significant catastrophe than a frivolous success. I think I'll stick to goodkindmanning.

Emma Jane was very cross to discover that Miss Pritchard had been at the lunch, since I have always told her that ladies are barred from these functions. She said that she wanted to come to the next one. I said she couldn't, and pointed out that Miss Pritchard, though a lady, happened to be a grown-up too; prepared, like a man, "to stretch her legs and talk the matter through". Emma Jane became crosser and asked me (irrelevantly) whether I had any plans to make money, so that she could retire. Like most liberated women, she wants to participate in male privileges without giving up any of those traditionally granted to women. If our roles were reversed, I said, what would she do for me that I didn't now do for her? What precisely was the magic ingredient that a kept woman brought to the deal? This baffled her. "That's different" was the best she could do. Pathetic.

*　　*　　*

Toby Danvers has ingratiated himself with Emma Jane by forcing Big Elaine to seek alternative accommodation. He did this by attempting to rape her. Returning, drunk as a goat, from a run-ashore, he wandered into her quarters and climbed, still in his galoshes and overcoat, into her bed. "Get off you big oaf", she cried, and caught him decisively in the boutique with her knee. Muttering that he had never been so insulted, Danvers retired to the sitting room and locked the door as a precaution against further assault. Big Elaine has now gone off to live among nice people in the Holland Park area. Quite right too.

Danvers, meanwhile, has taken possession of her room and has gradually collected from various addresses round London such material objects as represents a life-time of endeavour in the live theatre. These include a typewriter (the one, presumably, that he recently threw at the head of his last secretary); four shoes, non of which, unfortunately, makes up a pair with any of the others; a suit that appears to have moss growing on it; a collection of *Shit* posters, and a dog-eared filing system, which contains, among other gems, a nice exchange of letters between Danvers and Tory Party Central Office, in the course of which he tried to obtain money with menaces. Unless the Tories, he wrote, could see their way clear to paying him a considerable sum of money, he proposed to put them all back to square one by distributing the film of *The Christine Keeler Story,* which he had recently acquired. The Tories, to his surprise and indignation, told him, approximately, to get stuffed.

These new arrangements—which include myself brooding in the drawing room about pornography, Danvers dreaming in his room of the day he will prevail against his enemies, and Emma Jane dutifully subsidising our fantasies like a one-man Arts Council—would make for a very attractive life style, were it not for frequent interruptions and counter suggestions from my other new friend, Ken the Australian horse player. He's jolly nice and has pepped up our sex lives no end by pulling three girls a day and unselfishly popping them into our sauna bath (some are lovely, some hideous beyond natural justice, but Ken can't tell the difference—to him they're all molls), but, to my growing dismay, his suggestion that we open a model agency together has turned out not to be a joke, as I had supposed, but to have been made in earnest. Worse, he has duked the venture, as he puts it, by obtaining money from Farthingale. The likes of Ken the Australian horse player can smell a mug a mile away, and he promoted Farthingale, I've now discovered, while they were waiting to be treated at the clap clinic. Arrangements initiated on that occasion have now matured to the point where an account has been opened. in the name of Ken Pardoe Promotions, with Ken, reasonably enough, as the sole authorised signatory, at Farthingale's bank. This alarming development was a consequence of a visit to Highgate to call upon Farthingale's friendly bank manager, Mr. Pillock: a crushingly embarrassing occasion, in which I was foolish enough to become involved. Farthingale has no money at all, as it happens, apart from his weekly competence, but he has got considerable expectations: a fact that Ken had unearthed back at the clap clinic, and one that he now brought to the attention of Mr. Pillock with such force and enthusiasm that the good fellow caved in like a sand castle before the tide. In no time at all he had agreed to a facility of two thousand pounds, supported by nothing more tangible than Farthingale's guarantee. Since you couldn't open pussy on two thousand pounds, I wasn't too concerned at this point. I merely assumed that Ken would spend the money on various molls (an enterprise in which I might myself participate), leaving Farthingale to square the matter with his Daddy at some future date.

"Well Gentlemen, I must wish you luck", said Mr. Pillock, once the formalities had been completed. "May I ask whether you have yet acquired offices from which to run your business?"

This was a consideration to which I had not given any thought; and nor had Farthingale, judging by his stunned expression. Fortunately, Ken the Australian horse player was equal to the occasion.

"Blow me over, Pillock", said Ken, "we don't want offices.

No sir, we'll run the dodge from my lounge room. Have you tried to get an office recently? I've had enough experience of Estate Agents to last me a life time. They don't *want* to do business. Chestertons, Harrods, Knight, Frank and Rutley—they're all the same. Very polite and charming until it's time to close the deal—then, fuck me dead, it's a monkey on the table and they still want to look up your arse".

Mr. Pillock began to look a trifle faint and the notion that Chestertons and Harrods had now adopted this unusual method of taking up references caused me to laugh. But I stopped abruptly when Ken shot me a dirty look. Australians never say anything funny intentionally, so if you laugh they assume you're taking the mickey, and duff you up accordingly.

"I see", said Mr. Pillock, "so I assume that you will be running the business, Mr. Pardoe".

"Not on your nellie", said Ken, "No Sir. My job will be to pull the molls in off the street. The actual day to day will be performed by Mrs. Annoir".

Who the hell is she? I wondered, but I refrained from asking, since to do so might have indicated a lack of cohesion among the board of directors. Fortunately Mr. Pillock was in a better position to put the question.

"Who is Mrs. Annoir?" he asked.

"*Who* is Mrs. Annoir!" said Ken, as though scarcely able to believe his ears, "*Who* is Mrs. Annoir! Fuck me dead! Mrs. Annoir is only the shapest agent in town. Yes Sir. Smart as mustard, this one, and a really elegant broad, if you know what I mean. With her at the helm, we can't go wrong. You play your cards right Pillock you old scroundrel, and we might slip you one of our top molls from time to time".

Mr. Pillock looked aghast and muttered something about that not being necessary.

"Please yourself", said Ken cheerfully, "but don't bounce any of our gooses or I'll have . . ."

"Gooses?"

"Cheques—gooses necks, cheques. As I say, don't bounce any of our gooses, Pillock, or I'll have to hop round here and pull your nose. Ho! Ho! Ho!"

Shortly after this, Mr. Pillock ushered us out, and on the way home I asked Ken who Mrs. Annoir might be. I hoped she was a figment of his imagination, but this turned out not to be the case.

"Like I said, you old devil, she's the hottest agent in town".

"Do you know her?"

"Not yet, but I will. Yes Sir, I will".

God forbid.

*　　*　　*

God failed to intervene. Ken phoned yesterday to say that he was bringing her round to meet us later in the evening.

"But cock", he said, "excuse me for mentioning this, but no-er-you know, funny business. Get the picture? She's very straight this lady and she must think we're on the up and up. Don't misunderstand me now".

I understood him only too well. With sinking heart, I assured him that the flat would be cleared of all unsuitable people and that Emma Jane and I would play versions of ourselves unlikely to give offence at a debutante's tea party. By nine o'clock, this promise had involved us in a social problem of some trickiness, since Motor Show Polly, S. Z. Corbett and the doctor from the clap clinic came to call within minutes of my making it. Motor Show Polly and S. Z. Corbett, we regretfully decided, couldn't be relied upon to maintain the standard of decorum laid down by Ken as desirable on this occasion, but the doctor from the V.D. clinic set us a bit of a poser. Might not the presence of a professional man, one traditionally considered suitable to sign the backs of passport photographs and other forms, strike a note of stability and rectitude? In the end we ruled that discrimination would be wrong and that he too would have to go. We don't much care for him anyway. He is, as Polly warned, disgracefully randy—amazingly so considering how he spends his days. We only tolerate him because it tickles Polly to introduce him to habits, which, being a doctor, he ought to know are reprehensible. We told them to go and play with Dawn Upstairs until Mrs Annoir had been and gone. Emm Jane wanted to join them, but I flattered her into staying by pointing out that in the bad old days she'd been rather better at this kind of nonsense than I.

In the event, Mrs. Annoir was an agreeable surprise. She was helped through the door by Ken at half past nine, clearly the worse for wear. Ken, by way of explanation, said that they'd been dining well in the Edgeware Road. She was dressed, somewhat unfashionably I thought, in canary buttock yellow tights and what could once have been a trawlerman's jersey, stretched in the wash to achieve, just, the length of a dress. She wore a large floppy hat and such of her features as weren't hidden by dark glasses the size of motor cyclists' goggles looked kind, but rather coarse. Indeed her nose and lips seemed unnaturally swollen, like those of a middleweight contender with a cold in the head. The total impact brought to mind one of those beery lady jazz singers of the early fifties. We got through the opening pleasantries without mishap, and then she was sick on the carpet. Well, what a relief! Suddenly she seemed much less formidable, an impression re-inforced when she burst into tears and fell sobbing to her knees. Since she showed no signs of recovering her poise immediately, Emma Jane took her into Mr. Danvers's room and popped her into bed. If Mr. Danvers returned, she'd be a goner, but that would be all to the good.

"Hysterical broad", said Ken, who seemed to have lost a certain amount of respect for her over dinner.

"What's the trouble?"

"She's hung up on a no-good horse's hoof . . .".

"Horse's hoof? Forgive me".

"Poof, old cock, poof, Tight arsed little creep called Gregg Faraday. He's giving her a hard time, but what does she expect. Silly old moll".

I was immensely relieved that the sharp, elegant Mrs. Annoir had become a silly old moll, and hopeful that this crisis in her personal life might have an adverse bearing on our business plans.

"Oh dear", I said, "does this mean the deal is off?"

"No chance, old pal, no chance. In the morning she'll be as frisky as a two year old and champing to come under the starter's orders. Don't fret yourself. Your old pal Ken won't let you down".

That's as may be, but nor, fortunately, will Toby Danvers. Indeed any help emanating from Ken the Australian horse player can be smartly neutralised by assistance from that other quarter. After Ken had gone off for his nightly game of five card stud, Emma Jane and I evolved a plan. By the time Mr. Danvers returned to command module, the details of this had been well rehearsed. We took him into the living room, gave him a cup of black coffee and explained that by a curious chain of circumstance, too complicated to go into now, there lay in his bed, even as we spoke, an heiress of immeasurable means and surpassing attractiveness, but driven by sexual desires of a rather unusual nature. Only men with a true understanding of the live theatre had ever been able to please her. Naturally we had told her that such a man lived under our very roof, and she had begged us to become conspirators in the arrangement of her fantasy. All her life, she had said, she had dreamed of being ravished by a celebrated impresario. Might not Mr. Danvers turn out to be the very man to turn this dream into ecstatic reality? We had promised nothing, we said, other than that we'd put the matter fair and square to Mr. Danvers on his return, which we were now doing. If he thought he was man enough for the job, all he had to do was to strip naked except for his socks and boots, place Basil the Black Actor's bowler hat upon his head (this, we emphasised, was for some reason an integral part of the fantasy), present himself beside the bed in which she was pretending to be asleep, and proclaim the lines: "Good evening, I am Sergei Diaghilev and I wish you to appear as the dying duck in my forthcoming season at the Alhambra. Take your knickers off". She would appear to be very surprised, not to say petrified, but Mr. Danvers was on no account to be deterred, since this reaction of hers was all part of the scene. He was to perform a few dance steps around the room, as though demonstrating the choreography of the role he had in mind for her, and he was then to jump upon the bed. What happened after that was up to him, but bearing in mind that it was her fantasy to be raped, he must expect a certain degree of simulated resistance.

Mr. Danvers, as was to be expected, agreed to play the part, and dutifully rehearsed his lines while undressing down to his socks and boots. Once we were satisfied that he was word perfect, we placed Basil the Black Actor's bowler hat upon his head and pointed him towards his own bedroom. Though he closed the door behind him, he delivered his opening speech with such resonance that we could hear it with ease in the living room, and the ensuing thumps and bumps indicated that he had, as instructed, followed it up with a little dance. Then silence. For an hours we waited for an outraged Mrs. Annoir to emerge, screaming blue murder and threatening us with every kind of retribution, but nothing. So we went to bed.

She finally appeared this morning, while I was having my coffee. Suddenly the bedroom door opened and out she lurched, squinting horribly and seeming to walk with some difficulty : a circumstance caused, I realised as she stumbled into the living room, by the fact that she was only wearing one shoe. Her floppy hat was at a mad angle and her canary buttock yellow tights seemed to have lost definition in the night, so that they now drooped in baggy creases like a comic's in a pantomime. She stared in my direction with the pained, exaggerated concentration of a drunk, clearly trying to work out whether we had previously met. Then a beatific smile spread slowly across her bleary features and she spoke :

"Fantastic !" she said, "quite fantastic !"

She shook her head as though to indicate that one has no right to expect such experiences to occur more than once in a life time, gave a little wave of the hand, turned on her heel and limped towards the front door. Once she had gone, I went to expostulate with Mr. Danvers. He was sitting up in bed, looking unreasonably pleased with himself.

"My God, you were right", he said. "She really goes for that scene. I'm most grateful to you. I quite enjoyed it myself, as it happened. I felt a bit of a fool doing the dance, but her reaction made it all worthwhile. I'm meeting her tonight and I've got to go as Donald Albery. What do you suppose I should wear? Don't worry about the model agency, by the way. She's a typist with an import/export firm and has no intention of leaving".

*　　*　　*

A curious, though revealing, incident occurred on Sunday afternoon. I was watching the cricket on BBC 2 and Emma Jane was reading the *News of the World* with fierce distaste, when Ken the Australian Horse Player came through the door with a very pretty Portuguese girl he'd just gathered off the King's Road. She was considerably more attractive than most of the rough molls he's been turning up with recently—not that he can tell the difference, they're all Sheilas to him—and her manner was becomingly modest and dignified. She politely decline the soft drugs already in circulation, (Barry Richard's off-drive is something else again when stoned—me, that is, not him), explained that she worked as a secretary for a British company in Lisbon and that she was over here for a week's holiday, in the course of which she particularly looked forward to visiting York Minster and Salisbury Cathedral. Not much chance of jiggy-jiggy here, I was thinking, when Ken the Australian Horse Player plucked her out of the armchair in which she was demurely sitting, eased her out of her blouse, took down her trousers and screwed her on the carpet. During this unexpected episode, I continued to stare at the cricket and Emma Jane glared sternly at the *News of the World* with an expression that might have frozen the blood of Mary Whitehouse. After a while, the Portuguese secretary, purring like a fulfilled pussy cat, thanked Ken the Australian Horse Player for his attentions and said that she would now like a bath. Ken escorted out of the room and Emma Jane and I held a quick production meeting.

"Good God", said Emma Jane, "I simply don't understand how girls can allow themselves to be used like that".

"Nor can I", I said. "It's amazing. Can you imagine *any* circumstances in which you'd allow yourself to be picked up by a strange man, taken to a strange flat and screwed within minutes of arrival in front of a prim looking couple, one of whom was watching the cricket and one of whom wasn't?"

"I most certainly can't", snorted Emma Jane.

The point is we were both speaking with utter sincerity, yet a disinterested third party would undoubtedly say that criticism of Miss Portugal's behaviour came inappropriately from someone happy to go to bed with a total stranger so long as there was thirty quid on the table. "Typical of a whore's hypocrisy", such a person would say. "Emma Jane was merely shocked that a girl could behave like that without first submitting a bill".

This troubled me for the rest of the evening, because—although the hypocrisy charge seemed formidable—I did for once find myself agreeing with Emma Jane. I too had been sincerely shocked by Miss Portugal's behaviour. I was still brooding about this apparent confusion in our attitudes when Dawn Upstairs arrived in a terrible state, but quite unable to tell us what the matter might be until we'd given her a stiff smoke and two Valiums. Then it gradually emerged that her horrors had been brought on by the fact that she'd just had an orgasm with a punter.

"Oh fucking hell", she said, "I got it on and that, you know, and I felt so *ashamed*. I mean he was quite goodlooking and that, but *old*, you know probably forty at least, and anyway you don't want to think a gonk can make you come, do you?"

Emma Jane agreed that you most certainly didn't, and suddenly I had the solution to what had been troubling me. Dawn Upstairs's sad story made me realize that in her own eyes a whore is doing nothing reprehensible, or loose even, *so long as* she doesn't enjoy herself. So long as she is merely acting, her essential self, her moral self, is perfectly uninvolved. To criticise Emma Jane for being shocked by Miss Portugal's behaviour would be as wide of the mark as to accuse an actress, who was currently employed playing a murderess, of inconsistency were she to be shocked by a murder in real life. Were an actress presently employed as Lady Macbeth, say, to witness an assassination in her own drawing room, it would be silly to say to her: "Well really, I don't know why *you're* so upset, look what you get up to every night down at the National Theatre". To criticise Emma Jane for her suprise at Miss Portugal's behaviour would be as irrelevant.

*　*　*

I am making progress with my book on pornography. I have spoken with three pornographers so far, and have, in the course of the conversations, hit on an interesting new interviewing technique, which is to do all the talking myself. I put a question and if the answer fails to support my theory, I substitute the one I wanted.

I started with Big Elaine, but she persistently interrupted with her own views, which I found to be of negligible interest, and I became bored after about ten minutes.

Then I tried Emma Jane, but this wasn't a great success either. She refused to give the answers I required and I became cross. The interview ended after about twenty minutes with the pair of us sulking.

Next I spoke to Jill Rushton, a confident but pleasant lady, who ran the Lucy Clayton model agency for some years before moving to Peter Lumley. She was most co-operative and didn't in the least mind my calling her a pornographer. Leaning heavily on a recent article by Susan Sontag ("To be a woman is to be an actress. Being feminine is a kind of theatre, with its appropriate costumes, decor, lighting and stylised gestures. Indeed a woman who is not narcissistic is considered unfeminine. And a woman who spends literally most of her time caring for and making purchases to flatter her physical appearance is not regarded in this society as what she is: a kind of moral idiot"), I tried to get Mrs. Rushton to agree that models caricature the feminine role, becoming in the process female impersonators, hopping around with a bagful of props like Danny La Rue. Mrs. Rushton agreed that this was perhaps the case, but she didn't seem to think it mattered too much. She said she approved of model schools and charm courses, so I asked her whether she thought there ought to be academies of a similar nature at which men could acquire the manly arts. I had intended the question to sound ironic, but Mrs. Rushton didn't bat an eyelid. Yes, she said, she had thought national service a very good thing and would be in favour of its re-introduction. She maintained a similarly coherent argument throughout, which was most satisfactory.

Encouraged by this, I next interviewed Philip Hodson, the editor of *Forum*. Since I took him to be a serious man, I did quite a bit of research before this conversation, reading at least two copies of his magazine, and evolving, for his benefit, a special theory. I started (rather pompously, but what the hell) by trying to get him to agree that the proposition "the essential sexual nature of men and the essential sexual nature of women are different", must, if the law of excluded middle holds, be either true or false. If true, then *Forum* was wasting its time. By championing the right of women to enjoy sex, it was merely aggravating the innate incompatibility. *Penthouse* and *She* were more honest. If false, then *Forum* should redress some of the balance, publish female oriented erotica (like *Playgirl*), and most usefully of all, open a brothel for women. If it didn't know whether the proposition was true or false, it should devote its resources to finding out, and meanwhile cease publication.

As it is, *Forum* seems to embody a basic contradiction. While adopting a trendy, liberated editorial tone, every article in fact reinforces the suspicion that there is an unbridgeable gulf between a man's desires and a woman's. Nowhere is this better demonstrated than in a belligerent piece by someone called Marion Mead, in which she makes the scandalous pronouncement that a liberated woman "wouldn't pass up a stupid, good-looking stud for a lark". True, she goes on to repair some of the damage by saying that "the liberated woman prefers sex when love, affection or at least friendship is present", but one cannot help trembling for a world in which a woman *might* go to bed with a man simply because she found him attractive. In the same article she writes, "the sexual revolution of the sixties was mainly for the benefit of men, because in effect it encouraged women to feel guilty when they didn't readily put out". This alarming opinion—expressed by a self-styled liberated woman—unambiguously affirms that it is against a woman's true nature to be as sexually spontaneous, as self-evidently available, as a man might wish her to be. All that women gained from the permissive climate of the sixties, it seems, was a feeling of guilt if they failed to live up to male fantasies. If true, this is reassuring news for all pornographers, who can now continue with their well rewarded task of bridging the gap, without fear of competition from real, live, walking, talking women.

Forum, I said, was like an elaborate recipe for an omelette, written from the egg's point of view. Gourmets would be better advised to read *Penthouse* and *Experience*, in which the eggs at least pretended—for a financial consideration—to enjoy the process of being scrambled. Hodson said that I had acquired a very imperfect impression of what *Forum* was doing, and then proceeded to use up the rest of the tape expounding his own point of view. Since he used long and technical words that I couldn't understand and rattled out theories from the fields of psychology, biology and sociology, the validity of which I was not competent to judge, I was unable to interrupt. All very irritating.

I'm also trying to trap Michael White in my net, but he's proving most slippery. I took tea in his office a few days ago and tried to persuade him to agree to a taped interview. If he were willing, I said, I would ask him to defend *Oh Calcutta* against my assertion that it had a responsibility to satisfy the audience it had aroused, either by inviting them to mingle on stage with the cast, or at least by printing in its programme the telephone numbers of the more accessible brothels.

Success seems to have rendered him as enigmatically silent as Michael Codron, and he merely stared at me owlishly from behind his large horn-rimmed specs. After an age, he said: "Can you think of any reason why I shouldn't?" He looked most anxious, but what a question to put to me! (It reminded me of a lunch I once had with Michael Codron and N. F. Simpson. Codron and I had commissioned a play from Simpson, and the latter had come to lunch to collect our verdict. Codron maintained an oppressive silence through the soup and fish, and at last Simpson, on tenterhooks, could bear it no longer. "Well", he said, "what do you think?" Codron adjusted his expression to one even more impenetrably cryptic than its predecessor and said: "What do *you* think?").

I said that I couldn't for the moment think of any reason why he shouldn't, and so, looking very miserable, he agreed. If I cared to ring him in a day or two, he said, we could fix a convenient appointment. I thanked him and left, feeling rather unconvinced: a lack of confidence justified by the fact that he has now changed his mind.

I rang him this morning and he said he had decided that such a conversation would not at the moment be advisable. Pornography was a touchy subject and he thought it best to keep a low profile, as he put it, for the time being.

Michael White is, with the possible exception of Codron, by several light years the nicest and most intelligent person to have plied his trade as a commercial theatrical manager in the last God knows how many years, but really what's a prat! If he simply couldn't be bothered, I would quite understand. He's a busy man, arguably far too busy to waste an hour talking rubbish with me. But I don't think that's the problem. I really believe that he decided, after sober reflection, that the possible publication of any defence he might offer against my wholly assinine thesis would open a floodgate to spooky and unexpected dangers. It's a trivial matter, from his point of view, and I could be wrong. It's reasonable to assume that he only pondered the question for a few minutes and he might have thought: "Sod the fool, why should I waste my time? There's nothing in it for me". But I don't think that that's the whole truth. I believe his refusal is a symptom of the creeping cautiousness I detected in his manner over tea and one which must render life scarcely worth living. What a shame. He used to be good for a laugh or two. (He might argue, of course, that a little of the same creeping cautiousness on my part over the years would have saved him a few thousand pounds at times when he could ill afford to carry my obligations as well as his own. A cheap debating point, in my opinion).

*　　*　　*

News has reached us of an inquiry, conducted by Inspector Knights and Sergeant Mason (they sound like a pair of red-brick literary critics), into all aspects of the call girl business. It appears to have no connection with the one being carried out by the Old Grey Fox's firm, but follows the *News of the World's* latest lip-smacking revelations about various madames. So far, three girls who are known to us have been interviewed : French Simone, with whom Emma Jane has worked on a couple of occasions, Scraggy Janet and Pretty Marie. Apparently Knights and Mason are being very correct. They ring up first, are very polite and ask whether they may come round for an informal chat. They emphasise that the girls themselves have nothing to worry about, since they are in no way breaking the law, and that they merely want information about the three madames named by the *News of the World.*

Pretty Marie reports that they showed her a photograph that they'd confiscated after a raid on Bridget the Madame's flat.

"Is this you?" they asked.

"No", said Pretty Marie indignantly, "That's a grotty bird called Maralyn".

This has got back to Maralyn, and Pretty Marie's drawing room windows have gone for six again.

Emma Jane and Dawn Upstairs have become a trifle apprehensive, but I cannot see that there is any cause for concern. Neither of them has ever worked for any of the Madames involved, so I see no reason why either should receive a visit. And even if they do, they have nothing to fear, as Knights and Mason themselves sportingly point out. (Timmy Williamson, a student of police procedures since marrying into the business so to speak, has a theory that whatever the cops say, one should assume they mean the reverse. If he is correct, it means that if they say "I'm arresting you for such and such" you should reply "Oh, that's very nice of you, in that case I'll wish you goodnight" and walk away).

Emma Jane and Dawn Upstairs refuse to be entirely reassured. Like all call girls, they believe themselves to be on the wrong side of the law and there is nothing one can say to convince them otherwise.

Dawn Upstairs has gone so far as to prepare an elaborate alibi. "I shall tell them I'm a hairdresser", she says.

I point out that this is bloody silly, since the police will only call on her in the event that they know perfectly well what she is; if she tries to flim flam them, they'll give her a hard time.

"Oh dear", she says, "whatever shall I do, then?"

"Tell them you're a whore", I advised, "and ask them to mind their manners, unless they've got thirty quid apiece, in which case you'll mind yours".

"Oooh", says Dawn Upstairs, giving her Frankie Howard impression, "I couldn't say *that*. Whatever would they think?"

This sudden activity once again raises interesting questions concerning the Police's relationship with *The News of the World*. As with the Jean Horn/Norma Levy business, it is impossible to believe that *The News of the World* has printed anything that the Police didn't already know. With the possible exception of my Aunt Martha, everyone in London knew the names, telephone numbers and personal characteristics of the three Madames many years before *The News of the World* exposed them. It is a reasonable inference, therefore, that they have been operating all this time with police approval. This being the case, one would suppose that the police are very cross with *The News of the World* for blowing the whistle on a state of affairs that it suited them to sustain. Now they will have to do something, or *The News of the World* will print further crusading articles.

* * *

148

Over the years 'arding has spoken to me many times of his friend Stanley, who runs a dirty bookshop in Soho and once a month gives musical evenings in a garage behind Queensgate. Last night he escorted Danvers and myself to one of these, and very educational it was too.

Many of 'arding's friends are a trifle rough in their ways, and I felt rather apprehensive as we knocked on the appropriate door in a rather dingy mews: a state of mind not much improved by the immediate appearance of an enormous man with ginger hair and a button nose. He was wearing an old fashioned dinner jacket a size and a half too small for his vast proportions and he glared at us ferociously.

" 'Ullo Ginger", said 'arding, "remember me?"

"No", said Ginger, "can't say I do. 'Oo might you be?"

He glanced, with evident distaste, at each of us in turn, reserving an expression of special suspicion and contempt, it seemed, for Danvers. I was all for going home at this point, but Danvers smiled back cheerfully and was about to identify himself as the producer of "Shit", I thought, when 'arding said:

" 'Ere, don't wind me up Ginger. Stanley asked us".

" 'Ang about", said Ginger, and he closed the door in our faces.

Danvers was explaining that in a life time of attending social occasions of one sort or another, such a thing has never happened to him before, when Ginger reappeared with a tiny little man, who looked like a successful weasel. With a cry of joy, he folded 'arding to his bosom (or rather, since this was impossible due to a marked disproportion in their respective heights, he stuck his pointed head into 'arding's navel) and then rounded on Ginger with a snarl of rage. Had he been wearing a George Raft hat, he would certainly have taken it off at this point and, standing on tiptoe, used it to bat Ginger round the ears.

"You daft git", he said, "this is Johnny Harding's boy. What's the matter with you? I told you he was coming. What would Johnny Harding say if he knew you'd left his boy standing in the cold?"

"Sorry", said Ginger, hanging his huge head in shame and stepping aside to allow us to enter.

The inside of the garage had been done up rather well, and it now resembled a comfortable studio on two levels. The ground floor was large enough to have once housed six Rolls Royces, and at one end there was a staircase, which led, presumably, to a bedroom and the usual offices. Some twenty-five middle-aged men were sitting in a semi-circle, staring gloomily at a large cinema screen, which was not for the moment being used. In the space between them and the screen, a make-shift stage, which might have consisted of a few empty tea chests covered by a mattress, had been erected. Since we were expecting an orgy, the absence of women was rather a disappointment.

"Don't worry", said 'arding, as we took our seats at one end of the semi-circle, "the birds ain't arrived yet".

Stanley instructed Ginger to fetch some Spanish Claret for Johnny Harding's boy and his friends, and then, with the nerve-wracking optimism of a compere at a beauty contest, climbed on to the stage to deliver a vivacious little speech of welcome. During this, Danvers fell asleep and began to snore, and I carried out a closer inspection of our fellow guests. With the exception of a watery-eyed young man with a prominent adam's apple—the type you see eating alone at the Grill and Griddle or standing behind the counter at the Midland Bank—they were all past fifty and had the look of provincial dignatories. One had seen them, one felt, every few years on television, reading out the election results from Wolverhampton West and Billericay. 'arding saw me looking them over and assumed with his totter's mind that I was doing arithmetic.

"Two 'undred and fifty quid so far", he whispered. "Not bad for a start. Stanley charges them a tenner to get in and then scalps them for the rest of the evening".

Stanley wound up his little speech with a recitation recklessly entitled "Don't come home with the fish mother, sister's coming home with the crabs", which was received by the provincial dignatories with appalled silence ("amazin' " said 'arding, "bloody amazin' "), the lights were lowered, and a blue film of surpassing incompetence, starring two vicious looking schoolgirls and a tattooed sailor, appeared on the screen. Apart from Danvers's snoring, which I didn't care to interrupt, lest he attempt to strangle me, this, like Stanley's recitation, was received in total silence, with none of the dirty laughter and rude observations that you get when women are present. When it had run its course, Stanley, clapping hysterically like somebody's mother on a first night, jumped on to the stage once more and demanded to be told whether the provincial dignatories had ever seen anything hotter in their entire lives. The provincial dignatories stared back at him with the silent hostility of an audience at the Windmill, daring the comic not to leave the spotlight.

"And now", said Stanley, holding up his hands as though to silence on ovation, "and now we come to the high spot of the evening, the moment you've all been waiting for, a big hand please for the lovely Hilary and Linda".

He applauded himself into the wings—a vote of confidence to which the provincial dignatories failed to commit themselves —and his place was taken by two cheesey looking scrubbers— one black, one white—whose defeated bearing indicated a marked lack of sympathy with the circumstances in which they found themselves. The white girl, in fact, merely exuded an air of absentminded distaste, but the black girl wore an expression of pure horror, indicating appalled foreknowledge of what was to come. This apprehensive state of mind was adequately explained when the white girl shot her a perfunctory come-hither smirk, threw off her rather grubby negliee, revealing a long boney body, clambered onto the stage, lay down on her back and closed her eyes. With a last look of overt disgust, the black girl followed her on to the stage and collapsed on top of her. As their bodies touched, the white girl let out a moan of ecstasy that even Big Elaine might have considered unmotivated. The black girl shot upright as though electrocuted and Stanley came bounding on, applauding like a lunatic and begging the girls to tone down their antics, since the gentlemen could only be expected to take so much. Hilary and Linda, looking vastly relieved, recovered their negligees and scampered off back stage.

"How about that then, Gentlemen, how about that? Be honest. As a token of appreciation to the ladies, I'm now going to pass round the hat. I know I can rely on you to give generously".

With the huge figure of Ginger looming ominously at the back of the hall, his confidence that the provincial dignatories would endorse the entertainment so far in the most telling way possible seemed justified; and indeed the hat must have contained about fifty pounds by the time it reached us at the end of the row. I was going to add to this sum, but 'arding stopped me, insisting that Stanley had assured him that the evening was free. Since it seemed far from certain whether Ginger had been adequately apprised of all the terms and conditions of our participation in the fun, I protested, and during this small altercation Danvers suddenly woke up and took the hat out of my hand. "What a stroke of luck", he said, "I think I'll cash a cheque". He produced a cheque book (designated 'Shit' No. 2 Account) from his pocket, wrote out a cheque for two hundred pounds (the sum was unimportant, since the cheque was manifestly worthless; if Danvers had ever been authorised to sign on this account, the day had long since passed), dropped this into the hat, scooped out the money and pocketed it. It didn't seem likely that he'd get away with this for long, so I suggested that he put it back. Looking rather crestfallen, he eventually agreed to this, retaining a tenner, however, for himself. That seemed fair.

More Spanish Claret was provided, and after another brisk little pep-talk from Stanley, a second blue film was shown. In the course of this the dignatories were to be seen shuffling one by one to the back of the room and up the stairs. Each was absent for such a short time that I assumed it was the Spanish Claret that was causing the general restlessness, but 'arding put me right. It was the live show, apparently, that had unsettled them, and Hilary and Linda were now offering a further service back stage.

I think I'll go and investigate", said Danvers. He tottered away and was missing for about twenty minutes, during which time a queue of disgruntled aldermen lined up on the stairs. On his return, he said:

"Very interesting. I spoke with Hilary, the white girl. A charming person when you get to know her. They're charging a tenner for about three minutes. I offered her a cheque, but she's been too long at the fair for that. Told me to bugger off in fact. They're here on a free lance basis and Stanley guarantees them nothing. Furthermore, they have to give him 60% of what they take. In the course of the evening it is not unusual, according to Hilary, for some of the punters to make two or even three visits back stage. They expect to gross about three hundred pounds, which by my calculation means £60 for each of them and another £180 for Stanley. They're delighted with this apparently inequitable arrangement, since when not attending here, they patrol the Shepherd Market area, which is cold and less rewarding".

We left shortly after this, in full agreement on one point: that Stanley is on to a very good thing. So good indeed that we have decided to emulate him. If he can clear over £400 with such an uncouth entertainment, the sky's the limit, as far as we can see. It will be necessary, however, to leave Emma Jane's flat. It's too small for what we have in mind, and anyway she would never allow such an enterprise under her roof. We propose to say nothing at the moment, but we've formed an escape committee and an opening strategy has already been drawn up. We need a flat or house with three or four bedrooms and at least one large reception room. We expect the rent for such accommodation to be between £60 and £80 per week, and foresee no difficulty in obtaining such a place. The more expensive a furnished apartment is, the easier it is to come by, in my experience. Agents are only interested in their commission, so if you can slap a couple of months rent on the table, they can't wait to get you in. What you do after that is no concern of theirs. If you sell the furniture, knock down the walls and refuse to budge for another six months, that's the owner's problem.

We estimate that we need to raise an initial fund of £600. This, we feel, presents no problem. 'arding says he's good for £200 immediately, my share will be forthcoming from Lord Dynevor and Danvers says he can raise his whack from friends in the Turk's Head. (I have my doubts about this, but if he fails, 'arding and I can raise the required balance between us). This is very exciting, and already I can see that the book about pornographers is down the drain. And a good thing too. Its thesis was, after all, that pornographers should neither titillate nor advise, but *provide*. Stanley's little musical evening, for all its shortcomings, did more to free the provincial dignatories of anxiety and frustration than any number of girlie magazines or modish propaganda from *Forum* about mutual pleasure. Sod mutual pleasure. You don't go to a psychiatrist looking for mutual pleasure.

*   *   *

Second production meeting, attended by the entire escape committee, in a King's Road bistro. We can't use our flat at this stage, since I wish to avoid a confrontation with Emma Jane. Her paranatural powers of deduction have already made her suspicious that untidy plans are afoot, but fortunately her mind is rather on other matters at the moment. Knights and Mason's investigations into immorality have come closer to home and Emma Jane's name has now been mentioned. Yesterday they called on Black Danielle and went through her address book, Emma Jane is listed in this as Emma Compton, and when Knights and Mason saw this, they pointed out, pleasantly enough, that it wasn't Compton, but Crampton. This has made Emma Jane as nervy as a piano wire, and she and Dawn Upstairs are swallowing enough Valium to tide Roche & Co. over whatever difficulties they're presently having with the Government. Furthermore, to make the police look silly, they've given up eating and, more seriously, working. Every time the phone rings, they assume it's Knights and Mason and they drop it like a hot coal. All the other girls are behaving in the same neurotic fashion and the punters must be growing desperate (or, which is more likely, they must be visiting the escort agencies, massage parlours and the old boilers who advertise on notice boards. Since all these practitioners are controlled by gangsters, Knights and Mason, by harassing respectable call girls, are helping to subsidise the very elements Sir Robert Mark wishes to embarrass).

Since it would be foolish to find a flat suitable for parties before we have the money necessary to gain possession, the escape committee is concentrating at the moment on raising the initial capital. 'arding is standing by with his £200 and last night I rang Lord Dynevor in Wales, where the old fool is counting his sheep.

"This is your lucky day", I said, "we're back in business".

"Oh my God", said Lord D, "how much and where do I send it?"

"Two hundred pounds", I said, "but there's no panic. When you return to London will be soon enough". Bless him.

Danvers still maintains that his £200 will be forthcoming, but 'arding and I have our doubts. Such is his shortage of funds at the moment, it seems to us that he would have tapped his cronics at the Turk's Head before now, had he supposed that they would cough up. Never mind. Danvers will be invaluable in other ways. Since he has the most plausible front of the three of us, we have decided to take the flat in his name, or rather in one of his aliases. His lack of a bank account will be explained by the fact that he is a successful author, over here for six months to research a book, but resident in Spain. If I know estate agents, their eyeballs will click like cash registers when they see the six oh oh on the table, and they'll hand him the keys to their best property before he's halfway through his lies.

As to the form the parties should take, we are, at the moment, in slight disagreement. 'arding is in favour of copying Stanley's structure, with improvements, but a rather more ambitious notion is formulating itself in my head following reports I've received from Black Danielle about partouze houses in Paris. These are springing up like mushrooms, or so she says, and, catching the mood of the times, are catering to swingers rather than gonks. A basic rule of these places is that men can only attend if accompanied by a lady. The entrance fee is the French aquivalent of £10 and drinks are extra. Once inside there is no obligation to participate, but since the majority of the guests are self-styled swingers there tends not to be a noticeably inhibited atmosphere. According to Black Danielle, swoppers and swingers are flying from Heathrow to Orly by the plane load, so I see no reason why a similar enterprise shouldn't thrive in London.

Confirmation comes from Wandsworth Norman, who has been swopping his wife Rita her and there for many years now, and who tells me that London is lamentably under-supplied with focal points where people of his stripe can get it together. Consequently they are reduced to making their arrangements through the advertising columns of suitable magazines. This procedure is fraught with risk, it seems, because the couple from Purley advertising themselves as "Attractive, he 27, she 21, AC/DC, TV, Bon Flage, BBC, TT, keen to try anything, but *no* kinks", may, on closer acquaintance, turn out not to be up your street at all. (They might be Knights and Mason, of course, and then you're in trouble). (I don't know though). (Perhaps Knights and Mason . . . no, perish the thought).

It's a hit or miss business, but at a partouze house you can suss the situation before putting your chips on the table. And I feel that the legal aspect of such a state of affairs is more likely to confuse the authorities. If they raid the place and find nothing but stockbrokers and their wives, with not a whore in sight, they might be less sure of the relevant charges. I have by no means worked out a precise formula yet, but the answer might be to set up the North Chelsea Poetry Reading Society with an unusually high subscription rate. This would cover all expenses and would cut out untidy—and possibly incriminating—financial transactions at thed oor. The members would meet two or three times a week to disport themselves in any way that took their fancy. What poetry lovers get up to in their spare time is what poetry lovers get up to in their spare time, and no concern of the authorities.

'arding considers this formula to be too ambitious, but I think Danvers sides with me. In fact he agrees with everything 'arding or I say: an inclination that causes him to endorse two or three incompatible notions in a single sentence, and a further indication that he will not be a source of capital. The artistic elements in an enterprise always have to agree with the backers, even at the cost of contradicting themselves dizzy.

I take luncheon with Lord Dynevor at the end of the week, and to be on the safe side, I'll hit him for three hundred.

* * *

Lunch with Lord Dynevor. My nerve failed at the last moment and I asked only for the sum previously mentioned. He agreed to be standing by with this, against the moment when it will be needed. Things are shaping up nicely and the activities of Ken the Australian horse player represent the only continuing cause for concern. He's a delightful fellow, but exhaustingly persistent. He's now trying to find a replacement for Mrs. Annoir. His enthusiasm will be the death of me.

* * *

No it won't. The Yard have intervened on my behalf, lifting him on information received from Australia. This unexpected set-back occurred yesterday evening. Danvers was out on the town with his friend Mrs. Armstrong, and Emma Jane and I were enjoying a quiet rubber of bridge at home with Motor Show Polly and S. Z. Corbett. The phone rang and a strange, rather menacing voice identified itself as belonging to Detective Sergeant Turk. Since an unusually high proportion of our friends are heads, and since heads are notoriously given to whiling away the midnight hours with telephonic pranks, I assumed this was a joke. (Not a very good one, bearing in mind the jumpy state into which the activities of Knights and Mason have put us, and certainly not as imaginative as the celebrated example that has come to be known as the Stevie Holly special. This involves six people taking it in turns to ring up a complete stranger over a period of about two hours, asking to speak to Mad Harry. By the sixth call the total stranger has become hysterically tired of saying that he's never heard of such a person. "Well, tell him I rang", says each prankster, leaving a different name. Then the last person rings and says, "It's Mad Harry here, are there any messages for me?" and the total stranger's brain drops out. Tremendous fun.)

I replied, accordingly, with the old chestnut to the effect that I was selling tickets for the Policeman's Ball; if the person at the other end of the line couldn't dance, not to worry, it wasn't a dance, but a raffle.

That went down like a cup of cold sick, as Michael Codron, surprisingly, used to say, being greeted by an errie, creaking noise, like an ancient door groaning in the wind. I identified this as mirthless laughter and began to feel uneasy. Then Ken himself came on the line.

"Look, I'm in deep snooker here old pal", he said, "I'm being held at Bow Street. Could you hop over, do you think?"

Really, what a nuisance! And just when it seemed that Motor Show Polly and I were about to take some money off Emma Jane and S. Z. Corbett: no mean achievement considering that Motor Show Polly had only just grasped the need to follow suit —a requirement greatly at odds with her temperament. Furthermore, I wasn't too sure what being in deep snooker exactly meant, and since Ken's voice had lost none of its customary mettle, I assumed that he was being held on some trivial misdeameanour.

"Is that really necessary?" I asked, trying not to sound too grudging.

'It is, old pal, I'm afraid", said Ken, sounding more urgent now. "It's time to come to the aid of the party".

Grumbling somewhat, I departed.

At Bow Street, I announced my business and was shown into a small back room, in which, I surmised, many a member of the laity must have lost consciousness while helping the police with their enquiries. Ken, looking remarkably at ease considering the circumstances, was sitting at a small table, watched over by two gentlemen of exceptionally sinister aspect. One was immensely fat with piggy eyes, and the other was small and dark, with the cunning expression of a Welsh librarian. Ken introduced them as Detective Sergeants Turk and Evans and then explained the situation. Two years previously, he said, he'd "got his feet a bit muddy" in Australian and the law enforcement agencies of that country had now caught up with him. He'd been arrested two hours earlier in his flat on an extradition warrant. Fortunately, Detective Sergeants Turk and Evans had turned out to be men of the world and a deal of sorts had already been struck. For 'a twoer' they wouldn't oppose bail when he came up before the magistrate in the morning, and furthermore his passport and driving licence would now be entrusted to my safe keeping until he had need of them. I inferred that both documents would come in handy shortly. As for 'the twoer', this was to be contributed by Farthingale's friendly bank manager out of the Ken Pardoe Promotions funds. Ken now wrote out a cheque for the appropriate amount and handed it to me. It seemed that I would have to go to Highgate early in the morning, in plenty of time to return to Bow Street with the sweetener before Ken's case came up. I agreed immediately to these arrangements, not so much from a desire to help me friend as from a growing respect for Turk and Evans. They had said little since I'd entered the room, but both had the look of men to whom it would be wise to give 'a twoer' if in doubt. Turk and Evans nodded their heads approvingly at my decision, expressed their regret that they would have to detain my partner overnight and said how much they looked forward to doing further business with me in the morning.

I went home and explained the situation to Emma Jane, Motor Show Polly and S. Z. Corbett. After some discussion, it was agreed that I had done the right thing, but S. Z. Corbett's suggestion that I should carry out the financial transaction in front of an impartial witness made sense. It was decided that I would go to Bow Street in the morning accompanied by Toby Danvers, in case there was any funny business.

I got my twoer in the morning, but it was a close run thing. I woke Danvers up at eight-thirty and explained the situation on the way to Highgate in a taxi. When we reached the bank, I left him in the taxi, as a hostage against my non-reappearance, and presented the cheque with some confidence. After one of those embarrassing back-stage conferences, I was told that Mr. Pillock would like to have a word with me. I assumed that there was some technical difficulty of a trivial nature that could be ironed out by Pillock in no time at all, so, even though speed was of the essence, I wasn't too worried as I took my seat in his office. Bank managers can be exceptionally slow on the uptake, however, and I had to sit through the usual rhubarb before Pillock finally grasped the seriousness of the situation.

"I'm delighted to have this opportunity of a chat with you", he said. "I saw our friend Mr. Farthingale a day or two ago and he mentioned that he hadn't seen you recently".

"Indeed? How is Farthingale?"

"In the pink, I'm glad to say, in the pink".

"Good. The last time I saw him, he was a bit under the weather".

"A touch of 'flu perhaps? He seems fine now".

"No, he had the clap in fact. A very mild attack, but he thought the disease had spread to his kidneys, the silly sod".

I had a feeling that this was not the way in which one client of a bank should speak to the manager about another, but I was keen to get off the subject and down to the matter in hand.

Mr. Pillock looked rather startled.

"Oh-er, yes, I see. Well, no doubt the slings and arrows of er-ah-um . . . what?" He trailed off unhappily. "Anyway", he said, "I did want to have a word with either you or Mr. Pardoe about the state of the account. It does seem to be straying rather deeper into the red than we had at first anticipated, and I always think its best to rectify a situation before it gets out of hand. Do you not agree?"

"I do, I do", I said, trying to hide my astonishment that in a matter of three weeks Ken had, unbeknown to me, spent more than two thousand pounds.

"Now, let me see", continued Mr. Pillock, referring to a piece of paper on his desk, "at the close of business last night, the account had an overdrawn balance of £1,915. No credit payments have been received at all. Business a little slow, I expect?"

"A trifle, yes. These things take time".

"Of course".

"But the gooses should start rolling in quite soon now".

"Ah yes, the gooses. Indeed. Still, we did agree to a facility of £2,000 only. This cheque for two hundred pounds would take us over that limit".

"It's an unusual situation", I said, "you could say an emergency".

"Really? How so?"

"My partner is in deep snooker".

"Deep snooker?"

"Yes, a spot of bother".

"I'm sorry to hear this. Mrs. Annoir?"

"Er-no, in fact she's no longer with us".

"She's left? For good?"

"Yes. International politics, you know".

I had meant, of course, to say internal politics, and was about to correct myself when I realised that 'international' sounded more important.

"I understood", said Mr. Pillock, seeming to look still more troubled now that we were involved on a world-wide scale, "that Mrs. Annoir was to run the business. Surely her loss is a blow?"

"Not really. She turned out to be a silly old moll".

"Oh dear. Who is running the business now? Mr. Pardoe?"

"Not exactly. He's been arrested".

"Arrested?"

"Yes, last night. That is why I need the twoer. The two hundred pounds, that is".

"To pay some fine?"

"No, to bribe the police, as it happens".

Mr. Pillock sat back in his chair and stared at me in astonishment. For a moment he scarcely seemed to know what to say.

"To bribe the *police*?"

"Indeed. They've been very decent about the whole thing. For two hundred pounds they've agreed not to oppose bail this morning and they've already given me his passport and driving licence. It's imperative that I get to Bow Street with the money before ten-thirty. I really would be most grateful if you could see your way to helping on this occasion. I quite appreciate that the account is over the limit, but it is something of an emergency".

An emergency, the gravity of which Mr. Pillock still seemed unable to grasp. Instead of leaping into action, giving orders for the immediate encashment of the proffered gooses he continued to stare at me as though a stage weight had dropped on his head.

At last he spoke:

"You are *serious*, are you? I mean, you're not pulling my leg about this police business?"

He looked at me almost imploringly, obviously hoping against hope that I might be. I had to disappoint him.

"Indeed no".

"Oh dear, I hardly know what to say. Is Mr. Pardoe on a serious charge? Or perhaps I shouldn't ask".

"Quite serious, yes. Something to do with a nationwide fraud in Australia. You know what Australians are".

Mr. Pillock looked even more miserable.

"This is certainly a most unusual request", he said. "If I comply with it, I wonder if I am not aiding and abetting in the commission of a felony, or whatever the expression is". He gave a little wave of the hand, as though to indicate that until Mr. Pardoe and I became clients of his bank, he'd had no experience of these matters. "I find myself in a highly awkward position. I feel I ought to help, and I realise that the account is backed by Mr. Farthingale's very considerable expectations, but I rather wish that you hadn't told me the particular use to which the bank's money would be put. Oh dear, this *is* unusual".

He thought deeply for a while and then seemed to decide that bribing the police could be morally justified if the money came from an account that was guaranteed by a person with considerable expectations.

"I have to assume", he said, "that you know what you're doing". His expression indicated that this was an assumption he could only make with the greatest difficulty. "On this occasion I'm inclined to help, bearing in mind the sums of money that Mr. Farthingale will be receiving in the near future. But I must ask you or Mr. Farthingale to put the account in order as soon as possible".

"Of course".

"Good, good. Now, how would you like the money?"

"Perhaps it should be in notes of the largest possible denomination. I have to hand it over discreetly. The bundle should not be too bulky, I feel".

Mr. Pillock winced slightly at this remainder of the unorthodox purpose to which the bank's money was to be put, but he summoned a clerk nonetheless and told him to cash the cheque.

"I do trust", he said, while we were waiting for the proceeds to be made available, "that once this unpleasant business is out of the way things will look up for you. You and Mr. Farthingale will continue to run the agency?"

"Alas, that may be difficult now".

"I'm sorry. Are you thinking of entering another field? Something—how shall I put it?—steadier, perhaps?"

It crossed my mind to tell him of my partouze plans with 'arding but I didn't want him to think I was an idiot, so I improvised quickly.

"Yes, indeed I am. Much steadier, yes".

"Excellent. Might I ask what?"

"The laughter and heartbreak of the live threatre".

"The *live theatre*. My goodness me. A very chancy business, or so I've always understood. Have you any experience of it?"

"Not a lot, no. But I propose to team up with a very successful impresario called Toby Danvers. *Shit*, you know".

"Shit?"

"Yes, *Shit*. The musical. He put it on. He's doing immensely well. He's been in and out of mental hospitals rather a lot recently, but now he's as sane as you or I".

Mr. Pillock, who had risen to show me to the door, now sat

down again rather abruptly and passed a hand across his brow. I wished him good morning and departed with my twoer.

Inspite of Mr. Pillock's desire to chat, we got to Bow Street in plenty of time and joined the various elements, on both sides of the law, waiting uneasily in the main hall for the day's business to start. For Danvers it was like a school reunion and he seemed to know everybody. As yet there was no sign of Turk or Evans.

"My goodness", said Danvers, "there's Rudd. What a pleasant surprise. Over there. The shifty looking little man talking to the Irishman".

"He looks worried. I wonder what he's done".

"Oh, he's a solicitor and will no doubt be here in that capacity. I used him myself, as it happens, at the time of that misunderstanding over the cheque books. My family solicitors advised me not to instruct him on the grounds that it is one thing to have one's own previous convictions read out in court, quite another to have one's solicitor's. I used him, nonetheless, and am here to tell the tale, as you can see for yourself".

Rudd suddenly noticed Danvers and, seeming to abandon his Irish client in mid-consultation, came over to talk to him. Since there seemed to be a high risk of having one's pocket picked in this environment, I had kept my hand in my pocket guarding the twoer, but I now withdrew it in readiness for a formal introduction. Unfortunately, through some entanglement, I also withdrew the twoer, which fell to the floor, the drop causing it to disintegrate, so that the notes were strewn over quite a wide area. As I stooped to pick them up, I spotted the huge figure of Turk coming through the main entrance. He saw me and began to approach at speed. When he was only a few yards away he suddenly seemed to notice the wad of tenners in my hand and, imagining, I suppose, that I intended to straighten him here in the main hall, surrounded by officers of the court, he performed what was for such a large man a most impressive physical feat. Without changing the direction in which his body was pointing, he skidded sideways to the right, like Charlie Chaplin turning a corner, and, with an almost imperceptible movement of the head, indicating that I was to follow him, he disappeared up a staircase.

I found him, gasping for breath, two floors up.

" 'Ere", he said, "what's going on? I don't like the weight of this at all. What's Rudd doing here? Is he acting for your mate?"

"Not as far as I know. He happens to be an acquaintance of the person I'm with".

Turk narrowed his piggy eyes, causing them to disappear altogether.

"Came two-handed did you? I see. Got the passport and driving licence, have you?"

"No. They're back at my flat".

"Fuck. I don't like this at all, not at all. I'll need them. We'll have to forget the arrangement. Can you bring them down to the Yard?"

"I suppose so".

"Good. Okay, I can't stop here chatting now. Come down to the Yard in about an hour. Ask for me. Detective Sergeant Turk. And don't talk to anyone in the meantime, if you haven't already".

He gave me a nasty look before galloping off down the stairs. For such a bulky man, he really was exceedingly nimble on his feet: an attribute that had no doubt placed many villains—or those, at least, unwilling to give him a twoer—at an unforseen disadvantage.

I returned at a more dignified pace to the main hall, where Danvers was now alone. I brought him up to date and he asked whether he might be excused at this point from further participation in the proceedings. Things were rapidly becoming too exciting for him, he said, and if it was all one to me, he would now make his way independently to the Belgravia area, where he would occupy himself innocently until the Star Tavern opened. I reminded him not to be late on parade for our tea-time production meeting with 'arding and returned to the flat. I hung around here for a while and then took Ken's passport and driving licence down to Scotland Yard.

Turk met me at the entrance, and it was at once apparent from his manner that his attitude towards me had undergone a radical alteration: a circumstance brought about, I suspect, not from a sudden appalled realisation that he was dealing with a man of gravitas, but from an inability to rid his mind of a lurking fear that my connection with the mysterious Mr. Rudd was not as marginal as I had indicated. There was little doubt that their paths had crossed at some stage of their respective careers and that the experience had made Turk distinctly leery. He now greeted me almost fulsomely and as he escorted me up in the lift and down a long corridor, he gave me to understand that our previous arrangement had been a complete error of judgement on his part. Had he been in full possession of all the facts concerning my friend's misdeeds in Australia, he said, he would not, of course, have entertained the notion of a deal for one minute. He was only thankful that the other party to the arrange had turned out to be someone as intelligent, as upstanding and as honest as myself. I made suitably self-deprecating noises, but he would have none of it.

"No", he said, "no. Many people in your position would have behaved most foolishly. *Most* foolishly".

He showed me into a little office, in which the crafty looking Evans was sitting at a table. He shot to his feet as I entered, as thought I were the Commissioner himself, and arranged his features in an obsequious leer that was somehow more alarming than the expression of beady arrogance that he had worn throughout our previous meeting.

"I was just saying what an unpleasant business this has been", said Turk, offering me a seat.

"Most unpleasant", agreed Evans.

"And how sensibly Mr. Donaldson has acted throughout".

"*Most* sensibly", said Evans.

"And how we would never have considered an-er-um—had we known the gravity of the charges against his friend".

"*Never*", said Evans, replacing his obsequious leer with a look of scandalised outrage.

"However", continued Turk, "the passport and driving licence do present us with a bit of a problem".

"I have them here", I said, trying to seem bright and helpful.

"Good, good. But we have to explain how they have just come into our possession. In our report last night we said that they were not to be found on the prisoner's person or at his flat. Loose ends, you see. I don't like loose ends. You and Mr. Pardoe didn't have an office together?"

"No, I'm afraid not".

"Tricky, this one, tricky. Let's think".

"Why don't I just keep them?"

"No. We've got to produce them. And what's more we've got to say that you gave them to us today. But why did you have them, that's the difficulty. I think we'll just have to say that he left them at your flat by mistake and that when you heard of his arrest you brought them down here. I don't like it, but it will have to do. Would you be prepared to sign a statement to that effect?"

"Certainly".

Turk and Evans looked vastly relieved, and Evans began to type out an appropriate document. When I had signed this, they both escorted me back to the main entrance and, since it was now raining, Evans insisted that I wait inside while he braved the elements in search of a taxi. In his absence, Turk reiterated his opinion that I was the most intelligent, farsighted and honourable citizen it had ever been his pleasure to meet, and when Evans returned with the taxi, he held open its door and helped me in with the exaggerated deference of a doorman at the Ritz.

"Look", he said, "if you ever have any bother, get onto me. Know what I mean?"

So: I have made two friends for life, it seems to me, and I'm two hundred pounds better off than I was yesterday. Thanks to Turk and Evan's sudden coy refusal to be straightened, 'arding, Danvers and I now have the six hundred pounds we need to open our partouze house. What an amazing stroke of luck, a good omen surely! Even if Ken the Australian horse player beats the rap and regains his liberty (which seems unlikely, if Turk and Evans are to be believed), my claim to Farthingale's money is just as good as his. I introduced them after all, and Ken, up to the time of his arrest, had already enriched himself to the tune of £1,915. No, my conscience is clear.

Am I under a moral obligation, however, to tell Emma Jane of my windfall? After much thought, I have decided that I am, but that I will continue to keep her in the dark, nonetheless. I don't want her to know about the partouze scheme until it is nearer fruition, and if she were to become aware of my sudden wealth meanwhile, she could reasonably call on me to make token payments towards the upkeep of the household. I will have to hide the money, or better still, since Emma Jane is in the habit of going through my pockets when I'm in the bath, give it to 'arding until it is needed.

The incident with Turk and Evans is another illustration of the amazing audacity of bent policemen. When the Drugs Squad planted pot on me I was astonished by their impudent assumption that I, an apparently straight citizen, would not be nettled by their behaviour. So interested was I by this aspect of their work methods that I took the matter up with one of them during a moment of intimacy in the Gentlemen's cloakroom at Chelsea nick, whither we had repaired to wash off the finger print ink. (In order to protect the guilty, I shall call him D/C Don Juan.)

"Look here, D/C Don Juan", I said, "I'm a man of the world like yourself, and the last thing I want is any trouble. But you know that I know that that wasn't my piece of gear. How could you produce it like that and keep a straight face?"

"Actually", said D/C Don Juan, not in the least put out, "we were looking for something else".

"In that case", I said, "why didn't you bring it with you?"

" 'Ere, don't be like that, Charles", said D/C Don Juan, looking comically hurt, "that's not a nice thing to say".

Now Turk and Evans, by their willingness to be bunged by a total stranger within minutes of meeting him, demonstrated the same insane confidence, and, in the process, offered further evidence of the validity of Newman's law : the theory that corruption in the Metropolitan C.I.D. is a self-perpetuating tradition. Newman's argument is that a straight policeman, on finding himself in the C.I.D., has to have demonstrated immediately to his superiors that he is willing to abandon all inhibiting moral scruples, otherwise he will find himself back on the beat, with his record marked "unsuitable for C.I.D. duties". By this simple method, the C.I.D. ensures that good apples are tossed out of the barrel before they can endanger the bad. Backed up by such an efficient system, it is not surprising that individual detectives feel free to rip and tear with impunity. In these circumstances, the sheer *power* of a temporary acting probationary detective constable with five minutes' experience is perfectly terrifying.

*   *   *

Meanwhile, Knights and Mason have struck a telling blow at our already crumbling sense of security : they've called on Big Elaine.

They stayed for *four* hours, and since Big Elaine is incapable of spending ten minutes in anyone's company without divulging the most intimate details of her life to date, plus those of her friends and acquaintances, dwelling particularly on such aspects as might be thought of interest to the authorities, it is safe to assume that Knights and Mason now have in their possession all the facts they need to charge half London with conspiracy to debauch the other half. Big Elaine claims, in fact, not to have spilled the beans, but her report of what was said in the course of the visit is alarming enough.

It seems that Knights and Mason have got a list of more than two hundred call girls and it is their intention to visit all of them. Their primary objective, they say, is to collect evidence against the three Madames exposed in *The News of the World,* and against any others whose names crop up in the course of their enquiries. They also want to discover which girls are living with men, and they are compiling a list of illustrious gonks. They asked Big Elaine whether she knew Emma Jane and whether she had ever worked for Dawn Upstairs. She is adamant that she denied all knowledge of either, and on this point I'm inclined to believe her. Had she told them everything (including the fact that Emma Jane keeps a ponce), I believe her report to us would have been slightly different. She would have warned us, I think, that Knights and Mason had damaging information vis-a-vis ourselves, but would have implied that they had been in possession of this knowledge before visiting her. I have no reason to suppose that she feels malicious towards us, and I'm certain she would have marked our cards so that we could take whatever evasive action we deemed necessary.

The thought of the law spending four hours with Big Elaine is quite worrying enough, however, and a business girls' production meeting was convened in our flat at tea time today to discuss the implications. Had Knights and Mason been present, they would have been proud of themselves. The prevailing mood was one of mindless hysteria, such as you might expect in a chicken coop seconds after a hungry fox has come to call. Since

I was the only person present who was actually breaking the law (or any law, rather, that Knights and Mason were currently concerned to enforce), I took it upon myself to boost morale by fearless example.

Accordingly, I delivered a rallying little speech, in the course of which I rehearsed the same old arguments. Call girls were doing nothing illegal, I said; they held as respected a place in the community as did policemen (some would say more respected). This being so, there was no need to deny their profession to Knights and Mason. By concocting a ludicrous cover story, as Big Elaine had, they would deliver themselves, plucked and stuffed, into Knights and Mason's hands. Cops could smell a guilty conscience coming up the stairs, and if there was one thing they were good at it was tricking a person with something to hide into a damaging contradiction. Once caught out, the fabricator becomes demoralised and can henceforth be relied upon to sign a statement against his own grandmother. There was no point in their refusing to see Knights and Mason (though this was a course of action they were legally entitled to take), since by doing so they would keep themselves in the dark as to the course the investigation was taking. They should ask them in, be polite and admit at once that they were whores (since this didn't seem to come at all easily to them, I suggested that they spend twenty minutes in front of the bathroom mirror each morning, reciting over and over again: "I am a whore, I am a whore . . ."). If Knights and Mason asked awkward questions, such as "Is Dawn a Madame?" or "Where's the no-good ponce you live with?" they should look blank and say nothing. If Knights and Mason became threatening at this point, they should produce a notebook, head a clean page with the date and exact time, and say "Excuse me, would you mind repeating that last remark?" In the unlikely event that Knights and Mason continued, in these circumstances, to issue threats, they should excuse themselves on the grounds that they were going to A 10 to make a complaint.

When I had completed this faultless summing-up of the situation, Dawn Upstairs said: "I know, I'll say I'm a film extra", and Scotch Anna said: "I used to be a secretary. That's what I'll say I do".

I give up. The way the girls have played into Knights's and

Mason's hands is heartbreaking. Had they been organised from the start, the investigation would quickly have disappeared up its own backside. In fact they could have had tremendous fun: swopping identities, changing flats, talking rubbish, writing to *The Times*, marching on the House of Commons, blowing the whistle on the most unlikely people and carrying out a parallel investigation into the love lives of policemen's wives.

Unfortunately, call girls could never be persuaded into concerted action of this sort. Half are mentally unbalanced and spend their time shopping each other anyway, and the other half are so neurotically convinced they're doing something wrong that they fall apart before the first threat has come over the horizon. Someone stupid enough to believe that the police can expose an upright citizen in *The News of the World* is stupid enough to confess to anything.

I no longer have total faith even in Emma Jane. She is now in such a windy state that I believe she might crack if Knights and Mason probed in tender areas. If they were to discover that she has a ponce, for instance, and used this as a lever against Dawn Upstairs, they might, I think, get results. If they said "Look, Emma Jane, do yourself a favour. We know you're living with a man and we could get him into a lot of bother. Be a sensible girl and give us a statement saying Dawn's a Madame and that will be the last you hear of us. You might as well, *she's* given us a statement against you". If they were to spring this little trap, I think Emma Jane might step straight into it.

Sure enough, after the business girls' production meeting had broken up, Emma Jane burst into tears and said that she'd like me to go missing for a while. This was a bolt from the blue and I protested hotly. She didn't want me to do three years for poncing, she said. I pointed out that Knights and Mason either knew about me already, or they didn't. If they did (and gave a toss), I'd had it anyway. Even if I went missing now, they'd cop me eventually. If they didn't, we had nothing at the moment to worry about.

We have agreed, however, not to make their job any easier by drawing myself to their attention. Accordingly, we have packed up all my clothes and toys and hidden them, together with Danvers's, on top of the sauna bath. Should Knights and

Mason visit us without warning (not a piece of discourtesy they've so far stooped to), Danvers and I will take off our clothes and dance about as punters. (As Dawn Upstairs pointed out, rather cruelly, nobody would believe we were anything else anyway).

Unless Knights and Mason arrive with a search warrant—an unlikely eventuality and one that would mean we were dead ducks anyway—they'll find nothing untoward. If challenged as to my particulars, I shall say I'm a visiting fireman and give my address as c/o the Commissioner's son-in-law: a cover story that Tim and Christina will be only too happy to confirm. Toby Danvers will give his address as c/o the psychiatric wing of Westminster Hospital, his last permanent residence, as it happens, and one from which he was never officially discharged. (Sensing that the adjoining beds were all occupied by people suffering from diminished responsibility, he borrowed a fiver off each and beat it in the middle of the night).

Emma Jane has destroyed her bent telephone book and cooked up a new one in its place which might belong to the Queen Mother. She has hidden all the erotic photographs (and even unerotic ones of questionable people) and put in their place unexceptionable snaps of Lord Dynevor on his estates, knee-deep in cow flop and rare Welsh sheep, a charming family study of Timmy, Christina and their daughter Rachel which I took when they visited me in Ibiza, and a crumpled one, taken some years ago in our old flat, of Motor Show Polly and the rat. Why Knights and Mason should be impressed by this display of respectability by association, I'm not too sure, but it makes little Emma Jane feel less of an outsider. As a further precaution, and against my advice, she rang up my friend Scott to ask whether it would be in order for her to say that she worked for him as a part-time secretary. No, said Scott, it wouldn't. If questioned, he would be unable to tell a lie.

Since Scott is wholly good (compared with him Lord Dynevor —a saint by any other yardstick—is a sadistic monster from whom old age pensioners particularly should be protected), one of those people who volunteer assistance some time before you know you need it, and altogether faultless without being priggish or boring, I was rather impressed by this eccentric stand.

We spent a nerve-stretching evening in the course of which

Emma Jane jumped like a grasshopper every time the phone rang or there were steps in the corridor. Both she and Dawn Upstairs are convinced their phones are being tapped and they now speak to each other in an elaborate and sinister code, which would convince any eavesdropping bluebottle that they were at the very centre of a dangerous international conspiracy to bring down the free world. (Dealers in dope are afflicted with the same madness. "Er-hullo", they breathe, "is it cool to talk? It's er-you know who here. Can't say much, but I've got some er-um-*chocolate* here, know what I mean? Are you interested?" Such security measures might make even Slipper of the Yard suspicious that mischief was afoot).

At about nine o'clock Dawn Upstairs phoned, but the code on this occasion was so cryptic that even Emma Jane couldn't crack it, so Dawn came downstairs to explain in person. It was a job, thank heavens, the first for about a week. Two old friends of Dawn's wanted a couple of girls, but since neither she nor Emma Jane will allow her place to be used for immorality at the moment, they had to borrow a room at Wandsworth Norman's flat, for which the tight little sod charged them £15. I protested, telling them that they were mad, until it crossed my mind that this reluctance to use their own place was to be encouraged, since, if it lasts, it will be a source of income to me when I get my partouze house together. I shall undercut Wandsworth Norman by charging only a tenner for the use of a room.

* * *

Lunch with Scott. He said he hoped I hadn't been offended by his refusal to lie for Emma Jane. On the contrary, I said, it was a rare pleasure these days to meet a man with principles. I assumed that it was his Roman Catholic faith and the prospect of eternal damnation that prohibited him from telling Knights and Mason a small untruth.

"I'm afraid I have to disappoint you", said Scott. "Moral precepts played no part in my decision, merely prudence. Were I to lie, I'm convinced I'd be caught out and would consequently find myself doing time for perjury. I have no objection to lying as such, least of all lying to help a friend. In fact, I do so several times a day. Pure good manners. And to let a friend get into trouble would be an extreme example of bad manners. My reluctance on this occasion is caused by a simple conviction that I couldn't do it convincingly and that we'd all end up in worse trouble".

I was overwhelmingly disappointed. I had supposed that I knew *one* man at least who had an objective sense of sin, who made his arrangements not in accordance with prudence, but only after they had been checked against a hierachy of moral imperatives, in which telling the truth ranked higher than helping a friend. The discovery that Scott was a consequentialist like the rest of us came as a terrible blow, and I told him as much. He apologised for letting me down, but what can apologies do for a man who has had the morally confusing experience of watching the Pope perform the three card trick?

When I got home, I tried to explain Scott's point of view to Emma Jane, but it is not one she finds easy to understand, nor, once understood, easily condoned. I reminded her that game-keepers, paradoxically, are far mort fearful of the law than poachers, and that it is the law's ineluctable efficiency they respect, rather than any moral principles enshrined therein. To Scott, an untruth to the Authorities would represent the first step in an inevitable slide from respectability, involving immediate loss of wife, children, job, property and friends, to say nothing of the good opinion of his accountant, lawyer, bank manager and family doctor. Emma Jane was inclined to sneer at this almost mystical belief in retribution, and I had to point out to her that we would have shared it once. Game-keepers become poachers gradually; the process is so slow that by the time you have joined the hunted, you can no longer remember what it was like to be a hound.

"Bananas", said Emma Jane, "hounds shmounds. I've gone right off your friend Scott".

An unreasonable decision, in my opinion. If he thought the situation was serious, he'd be the first to help.

* * *

Knights and Mason have struck again, and lethally. This afternoon they called without warning on Scotch Anna.

"She was sat in the hall was Anna", Dawn Upstairs reports, "giving Pretty Marie a job down the phone. There's a ring on the front door, isn't there, and Scotch Anna, thinking it's the television repair men, lets them in and goes on talking to Pretty Marie in front of them!"

Caught bang to rights, Scotch Anna nonetheless stuck to her secretarial alibi and, when Knights and Mason said they'd visit the school which her son attends, proclaiming themselves to be the Vice Squad unless she made a statement against Dawn Upstairs, she pluckily told them to bugger off.

This they eventually did, but Emma Jane has gone into an irreversible tailspin and I'm not feeling too clever myself. Knights and Mason's new procedure of calling without warning is most unsettling and, in spite of my courageous words, I'm not too sure that I could bring myself to open the door to them, were they to turn up unexpectedly. Accordingly, Danvers and I have moved out temporarily and have come to live with Christina and Tim at 14 Elaine Grove (no relation, as far as I know). Being on the run from the police is rather exciting, I find, and holed up with Tim and Christina seems to be as good a place as any. There are other advantages too. For one thing Christina is a lovely cook, and being beyond the reach of Emma Jane's authoritarian eye means that Danvers and I can spend the days looking for a suitable partouze house without her wondering what we're up to.

Over dinner tonight we devised a scheme to make the *News of the World* look silly. An intermediary—Danvers for instance —will ring up the *News of the World* and say: "It so happens that I might be in a position to put a little story your way, not unconnected with your present fearless investigations into the call girl business. Thirty-eight year old *Beyond the Fringe* ship-owner's son William Donaldson has been living as a ponce for the last year at the very centre of London's biggest vice-ring. Now, for five pounds, he is prepared to reveal all. Furthermore, Emma Jane, the girl he's been poncing off and well known as one of London's most shameless courtesans, is likewise ready to spill the beans. If you're interested, I can produce the two of them in a pub in Belsize Park tomorrow, but no funny business".

The *News of the World* would check around a bit, I'd guess, and they'd easily discover that there might be a modicum of truth in the story. Accordingly, they'd agree to a meet. Danvers would go to the put with two people whom he'd introduce as Willie and Emma Jane, but who would in fact be Timmy and Christina. Tim and I look alike anyway, and he knows quite enough about the details of the business to convince a couple of drunken *News of the World* reporters that they were authentic. In the absence of any evidence to the contrary, I see no reason why a reporter should suspect that someone blowing the whistle on himself is not the person he says he is. (This switch of identity notion first occurred to me during one of my difficulties a couple of years ago. On that occasion, some common little body from The *Daily Express,* high on her excitement at having cornered me, began to insult me through my own letter box without first checking on whether I was the person she thought I was. For all she knew, I'd come to sell insurance). Anyway, the next Sunday, the *News of the World* would print a gruesome confession entitled "Our life by vice, by the Producer of *Beyond the Fringe* and Emma Jane", above a photograph of Christina and Timmy. Whereupon Emma Jane and I, who had been spending a quiet week in Norfolk with her parents, would appear, in a very hot and bothered state, to protest. I tremble to think what the damages would be. £100,000? More? Talk about loss of reputation. Tim is very keen to launch this little joke, but Christina is not confident that she could adequately play the role of a tart. True, no one would mistake her for a brass, but nor would they Emma Jane. We also wonder whether such a jape might not be constructed as conspiracy to defraud. I could fail to sue, of course, in which case fraud wouldn't come into it, but doubtless the authorities would still get us for skylarking or some such disruptive misdemeanour. We might do it nonetheless.

*   *   *

Lunch with Lord Dynevor. He thinks (as does Tim) that my going into hiding is an over-reaction. (Tim actually thinks it's a way of making myself seem more important, which is highly irritating).

"Now look here", said Lord Dynevor, "poncing's a very *extreme* charge".

In his neck of the woods it very well may be, I said, almost unheard of in fact, but this regrettably was not the case in my milieu. My acquaintances, indeed, were currently going down like ninepins before this very accusation.

Lord Dynevor remained unconvinced. The trouble is that people like him and Timmy are simply incapable of *imagining* a friend of theirs caught up in such an outlandish context. To them a ponce is a scar-faced Cypriot who hasn't worked for twenty years, and they would expect such a person to be carted off in a trice. Lord Dynevor admitted that this was the assumption behind his thinking, but he suggested that it was also behind the police's. He might be right at that, but if so, how outrageous.

I told him of Scott's unexpected refusal to fib for Emma Jane and of my disappointment when I discovered that his reservations were not moral but practical. He agreed that it was no longer easy to identify with people to whom the infringement of one rule entailed catastrophe. Not a law breaker himself, it was in the field of sexual infidelity that he now had difficulty in remembering the sense of inevitable downfall that had accompanied his first lapse. His position now, he said, was somewhere between mine and Scott's. He would certainly perjure himself to protect a friend, he said, whatever the friend had done, but he would insist on doing it his way (I tremble to think what this might be). Would he lie to protect one friend from another? I asked. Were Tim to burglarise his house, for instance, would he, Lord Dynevor, think I was obliged to tell him?

He agreed that I wouldn't be, that in such a case my responsibility would be to keep Tim out of trouble rather than to protect Lord Dynevor's ill-gotten gains, on the grounds that Tim would suffer more by going inside than Lord Dynevor would by losing a few family trinkets and a couple of rare sheep. He felt, however, that there must be a point at which Tim should rightly be discouraged. If he robbed all his friends' flats, for instance, one after the other. On the whole, however, he agreed that the worst sin was to hand a wrong-doer over to the authorities. This code is the conditioned reflex of a gangster and that I've come to embrace it so completely rather troubles me.

Lord Dynevor gave me a cheque for £200 and after lunch I took this round to 'arding, together with the 'twoer' originally earmarked for Turk and Evans and still, miraculously, intact. We are now capitalised and tomorrow we shall start looking for flats. We have decided that I shall front the operation after all, since the bottom has just fallen out of Danvers's best pair of trousers. At first we tried to patch this up with an old copy of the *Daily Mirror*, as dossers do, but we felt that he might rustle rather and make estate agents leary. I shall make my calls with Mrs. 'arding as my wife, since married couples are traditionally supposed to be more stable in their ways.

* * *

This business of getting flats is, as I'd always supposed, a doddle. I can't think why people make such a fuss about it. So long as you're prepared to pay seventy or eighty pounds a week, they're a steal. It seems as if we've got one already and it's perfect. This morning we rang up a debby-sounding egg who advertises herself in *The Times* as 'Elegant Homes Limited' and this afternoon she took Mrs. 'arding and me round four flats, any one of which could have suited us excellently, but the last was designed as if with us in mind. Situated in a small discreet block at the affluent end of the Fulham Road, it consists of four large bedrooms and a double drawing room with sliding doors. This device will provide a ready made stage for tableaux and surprises of all sorts. It is furnished and decorated according to the heavy, sensible taste of the retired Major General, now living in Dorset, who owns it.

Mrs. 'arding got so stuck into her role that for a moment I was afraid that she was going to lose us the place through being over-critical. I'd instructed her to ask intelligent, family questions like "Where's the airing cupboard?" and "is there a washing-up machine?" but she got carried away and kicked up something dreadful about there not being a heated towel rail in the bathroom.

There was an awkward moment too in the master bedroom when I made some observation to Mrs. 'arding about which side of the double bed each of us would claim and she, forgetting her role, shot me a look of undisguised horror and said something like "You'll be lucky".

No doubt Miss Hunter-Forsyth, the debby estate agent, mistook this exchange for a piece of marital skittishness: a lesson learned from the sex educationalists who advise wives to keep their husbands on their toes by being mysterious and, from time to time, girlishly unavailable.

Whatever she thought, she turned out to be a pushover when I said I'd take the place. In fact, when I told her my story—writer resident in Spain, over here to research a book on police corruption, no bank account in England, tax evasion you know, have to be cash on the table—she became frightfully excited and almost said that she *preferred* people without references. As it happens, I am not completely without these. I've given Tim as my literary agent—he used to be an agent, after all, and still has some of the appropriate writing paper—and Lord Dynevor (Miss Hunter-Forsyth thinks the old fool may have attended her coming-out dance) as my character witness. The matter is now a mere formality, she says, and, best of all, she only wants one month's rent in advance, plus a deposit of £100. The flat is eighty pounds a week, so I've only had to cough up £420. This means we have £180 with which to finance the first partouze.

This evening, Mrs. 'arding and I gave 'arding a report on the place, during which it became apparent that Mrs. 'arding, in the course of our inspection, had carried out a most thorough and professional valuation of the furniture, fixtures and fittings therein. I became a trifle nervous and suggested to 'arding that the place should not be stripped unless, and until, the partouze scheme turned out to be a floater. He agreed to this, but expressed slight concern that the flat is a mere fifty yards from Chelsea nick. This is pushing our luck slightly, he thinks. I disagree—on the double bluff theory—and consider the situation analagous to the story about the well-known thief who joined a construction gang. Each night he was to be seen pushing a wheelbarrow full of straw away from the building site. Each night a policemen stopped him and searched under the straw.

Nothing. When the job was completed, the exasperated cop said: "Come on Lefty, you can own up now. What were you nicking?" "Wheelbarrows", said Lefty. (Now I've come to write it out, I can no longer see what the connection is, but there you go).

According to the delightful Miss Hunter-Forsyth we can have the keys in a day or two, and I haven't been so excited for years.

*　　*　　*

A scandalous story is circulating among business girls and their connections concerning Knights, Mason and Big Elaine. This is to the effect that the well-known police technique of stripping suspects naked before interrogation has not worked in her case. Summoned to Saville Row, she was taken into a small back room and told, so the story goes, to take her clothes off. This she did, whereupon the interrogating officer confessed to three bank robberies, a hijacking, two long firm frauds and seventeen other offences which he wished to be taken into consideration. A disgraceful slur, in my opinion, and one in which there is not a grain of truth.

*　　*　　*

I've confessed my scheme to Emma Jane and she hardly knows what to think or how to react. In fact she finds herself in an uncomfortable dilemma. She's disconcerted at this sudden change in my arrangements, but since she's been going on at me for weeks to get myself together, she can't come on too strong. Today I showed her round my new accommodation and she was impressed despite herself. Not by my plans, however. Indeed she is quietly confident that I'll fall on my arse.

"Don't be daft", I said, "How is it possible to lose money on a brothel?"

"You'll find a way", she said.

If she's right, this at least will make a good defence when I'm up for living on immoral earnings. You can hardly be guilty if there aren't any. I have asked her to participate in the partouzes, but she has declined the offer. In fact she is being very dignified and sniffy about the whole thing. Her goodness is infinite, however, and since the Major General has failed to equip the place with a television set, she's lent me one of hers. I'll not miss *Match of the Day* for the best partouze yet thrown.

* * *

Danvers and I have moved in. The excitement has proved rather too much for us and for the first week we have done nothing except luxuriate in our new and lush surroundings. We've also managed to spend most of what is left of our initial capital (mainly on refreshing Danver's Irish friends from the Turk's Head, some of whom are writing novels, and some of whom aren't) and this circumstance has finally compelled us to set the first partouze for next Friday.

Unfortunately, it now turns out that I don't know any swingers apart from Wandsworth Norman and his wife Rita (and he's too mean to pay—comically desperate though he is) and such of Danvers's many acquaintances as are still young enough to remember what it's for are far too drunk to get it together.

'arding, at least, has come up with one couple : a charming stockbroker and his wife, to whom he recently sold some furniture. They're called Mr. and Mrs. Renwick, and 'arding brought them round last night for an audition. I think we all passed with flying colours. They promise they'll come on Friday and they intend, furthermore, to bring another couple with them. They are, I'd say, exactly the sort of people we're looking for. If Friday's to their liking, the word will be through the Stock Exchange on Monday morning like a plate of figs, and thereafter it will be striped shirts, elastic sided boots and chicken on Sundays for 'arding, Danvers and me. Mr. Renwick is very tall and goofy and Mrs. Renwick is rather attractive after the fashion of the cool ladies to be seen taking tea with a girlfriend in the Soda Fountain at Fortnums or the Health Juice Bar at Harrods. They're in their early thirties, I'd suppose, and disarmingly candid about their non-participation to date in the looser pleasures of the permissive society. Mrs. Renwick has got her eye on 'arding, I'd say, and as he offered a little trailer of the joys to come (" 'Ere", he said to Mr. Renwick, *"Mad* birds will get 'old of you . . .") she crossed her legs and began to melt visibly like an iced-lolly on a June afternoon. She has worked out, no doubt, that if the only way she'll get 'arding is at a partouze, then it is at a partouze that she'll get him. Mr. Renwick, I'd think, is merely randy, no more no less; and to organise something on the side would be beyond his capabilities and marriage vows.

Still, having advertised ourselves as the people who can really make it happen, we won't grow rich and famous by introducing one couple to another they already know and by charging them ten pounds each for the use of our hall; accordingly, we have made certain other arrangements that strictly speaking go outside our original formula. Wandsworth Norman and his wife Rita are to be allowed to attend free on condition that they bring with them one other paying couple. This, Wandsworth Norman assures me, they can do. We have also informed certain single men that they can come on their own, but that the penalty will be an entrance fee of twenty pounds. Finally, we have booked Dawn Upstairs and Scraggy Janet to come as wives and to act as catalysts should the proceedings not be going with a bang.

Since none of the management has ever attended an occasion such as the one we have in mind, we have no idea what might be needed to get the show on the road. In the circumstances we think it prudent to have a couple of reliable professionals planted discreetly among the amateur fun lovers, even though such a strategem is almost certainly contrary to the spirit of the game. Dawn Upstairs and Scraggy Janet are charging a hundred pounds for their services, so I hope very much that someone else turns up.

* * *

FIRST PARTOUZE. Wake up late (11.30) having had a bad night. Couldn't get to sleep until four or five this morning. First night nerves, no doubt.

11.45

Totter round the flat in search of Danvers. Find him eventually under the dining room table, fully clothed with an empty bottle of scotch beside him. Wake him gently and remind him that we're back in show business. Give him a cup of coffee and convene first production meeting.

12.00

First production meeting. Concentrate at first on the stage management aspect and how best to dress the set. Danvers in his element now, manifestly happier than he's been at any time since the final dress rehearsal of *Shit* in a tent in Holland. Wishing to avoid at all costs a stiff, cocktail party atmosphere and feeling that even the most dedicated and experienced swoppers will be more likely to trade uninhibitedly in noticeably undomestic circumstances, we decide to create as far as possible the anonymously sleazy tone of a night-club: an atmosphere in which perfectly respectable people traditionally behave in a more uncouth fashion than they would ever dream of doing in a friends drawing room.

Accordingly, we decide that such of the Major General's furniture as does not seem likely to lend itself to spontaneous swinging will be placed in store. We ring 'arding at his place of work and he says that this can easily be arranged later in the afternoon. A friend of his will come round with a lorry. Still in accordance with the intended night-club motif, we then decide to construct a kind of cash desk at the front door, over which 'arding, as the most businesslike of the management, will preside. Once past this, the punters will be left to their own devices, uninhibited by the hovering presence of a nervous host and hostess, hysterically determined that their guests shall have a good time. They will have to find their own way to a bar that we'll erect in the dining room, operated—while still sober— by Danvers. By the time he's too drunk to pour the drinks, the punters should feel sufficiently at home to help themselves.

Finally, since I can never believe that swoppers really want to get a clear view of one another, we decide to put red bulbs of a remarkably kind wattage into all the lamps. Since we have no red bulbs on the premises, Danvers volunteers to go out and purchase some. I twig that this is no more than a rouse to catch the saloon before they close and accordingly veto the suggestion.

12.45

Draw up a projected profit and loss account based on the situation as it looks at the moment.
On the credit side :

Balance of initial capital	£30
Potential income	
Mr. & Mrs. Renwick	£10
Friends of same	£10
Friends of Wandsworth Norman	£10
Ricky the Restaurateur	£20
Ruislip Terry	£20
Ossie in Dry Cleaning	£20
	————
	£120

On the debit side :

Drink, red bulbs, bits & pieces	£40
Salaries to Dawn Upstairs &	
Scraggy Janet	£100
	————
	£140

A net loss of twenty pounds, even if everyone turns up. Catastrophe. Ring Dawn Upstairs in a panic and she says "Don't worry I can get as many punters as you like". I tell her that two or three's enough. We don't want the men to out-number the women too noticeably. We're in the wife swopping business after all and we don't want the genuine wives to get jumpy.

1.30—2.30

Break for lunch. Danvers wants to repair to a pub, but I insist on fish and chips from the corner shop. There's work to be done yet.

2.45

'arding arrives with his friend Terry in a removal van. The Major General's more inappropriate furnishings disappear, possibly never to be seen again. Terry has a twinkle in his eye. Once the huge dining-room table has been disposed of, we turn

the area thus reclaimed into a kind of stage on which 'arding
and Dawn Upstairs will suddenly go the other way if the proceedings are going sluggishly. We then erect the bar, and the
turnstile at the front door.

3.15—4.00
Management lie-down, made necessary by so much unaccus-
tomed labour.

4.00
Danvers despatched, now the pubs are closed, to purchase the
red bulbs.

4.15
Dawn Upstairs rings to say that she's got three more punters at
£20 a head: Old King Cole, an immense and insatiable spade,
Larry the Racing Driver and Bobby in Baby Clothes. She warns
us that the Viscount is endowed beyond the point of reason and
that neither she nor Scraggy Janet can be relied upon to accommodate him.

We appear to have got ourselves out of a financial jam, but
only by unbalancing the numbers badly. If everyone turns up
who promises to do so, the breakdown is now six women (Mrs.
Renwick, Mrs. Renwick's friend, Wandsworth Norman's wife
Rita, Rita's friend, Dawn Upstairs and Scraggy Janet) to thir-
teen men (Mr. Renwick, Mr. Renwick's friend, Wandsworth
Norman's friend, Ricky the Restaurateur, Larry the Racing
Driver, Viscount Swingler, Bobby in Baby Clothes, Ruislip
Terry, Ossie in Drycleaning, 'arding, Danvers and I—not that
you can count me and Danvers, except an unnecessary ballast).

Such an imbalance is clearly dangerous and I courageously
ring up Emma Jane to ask whether she would consider making
a special guest appearance for charity and she says bugger off
and hangs up on me. Can't say I blame her.

5.00
'arding unselfishly suggests that Sarah attends instead of him.
(They can't both come because someone has to stay at home to
look after their son James). This is a tricky one. 'arding, being
young and pretty, would undoubtedly be an asset, possibly the
only man present any wife still with her faculties and eyesight

could possibly find attractive, but Sarah in the circumstances would be even more of an asset. Eventually we agree that Sarah's the answer and this improves the situation somewhat. It's now twelve men to seven women, or ten to seven if Danvers and I keep out of the way, which is my intention at least. This balance is okay, I think.

5.45

No it bloody isn't. That little prat Wandsworth Norman rings to ask how things are going.

Quite well, I say, and then I ask him to confirm that his couple are coming.

Certainly he says.

Good, I say, what are their names?

"George and Fred", he says.

George and Fred! Whatever next? Which one's the girl?

"Girl?" says Wandsworth Norman, "Girl? Neither of them".

"Goats and monkeys", I say, "I specifically said you had to bring another couple".

Well, says Wandsworth Norman, they are a couple. Two. A pair. A brace. I made no specifications, he insists, as to sex.

God Almighty, what class of person were they then?

Oh, says Wandsworth Norman, a very good class. One was his chauffeur in fact and one a plumber.

A plumber and a chauffeur! What will Mrs. Renwick think? Eventually I say he can still bring them but that each will have to pay £20. The tight little sod protests, but at last agrees.

6.00

In the light of this blow we draw up another balance sheet to see whether we can afford to pay for more girls. (Otherwise we'll be back to square one). The possible gross income is now £180 which should represent a profit of £40 if everyone turns up. The question is whether to spend this on another professional girl and risk having no capital for a second partouze, or leave things as they are and risk an artistic disaster so that no-one turns up for the second night even if there is one.

Debate the matter for an hour and get nowhere. I'm for spending the money, but 'arding and Danvers are for holding on until we see who turns up. They point out that two or three of the punters have only to drop out for us to look really stupid. This is becoming nerve-wracking. Danvers and I exchange our first cross words. More first night nerves.

7.00
We go out to buy the drinks. Danvers ricks his back on way home and retires to his bedroom.

7.30
'arding departs to switch stations with Sarah.

8.00
Sarah and Dawn Upstairs, both of whom have sportingly agreed to attend the final technical run through, arrive at the same time. I fill them in on the balancing problem and they, being girls, feel threatened and not unnaturally side with me.

Dawn Upstairs produces the solution. She knows two little girls, she says, who are only just starting in the business, and she thinks she can persuade them to come as topless waitresses for a tenner each. One at the door and one behind the bar. They'll inevitably get roped in and we'll have two extra girls for only twenty pounds. This makes sense and Dawn Upstairs makes the appropriate arrangements down the phone.

8.15
I walk Dawn Upstairs round the set and explain her duties. I emphasise that we are running a wife swopping establishment, not a meeting place for gonks and naughty girls, and this being so, it is of primary importance that the Renwicks and their friends are impressed. The unaccompanied gonks must be made to understand that this will be the only occasion on which they'll be allowed to enter without a girl. Dawn and Janet must in no way behave like professionals. Since she must seem to be a wife, which gonk does she wish to pair herself off with?

She thinks for ages, comparing the various qualities and defects of each. Eventually I have to tell her not to go to pieces, it's only for one evening, not for the rest of her life. At last she decides on Larry the Racing Driver. I then remind her that, since it will be her job to be the most uninhibited of the wives, she will have to get hold of someone else's husband if things are going slowly. This causes her to switch horses, choosing Bobby in Baby Clothes as her husband so that she can get hold of Larry the Racing Driver.

8.30

Put out the drinks. Notice that a bottle of whiskey is missing and go to look for Danvers. Find him snoring in his bedroom with the missing bottle half empty beside him. Decide to leave him where he is and to make his bedroom out of bounds. There could be problems if he wakes up.

9.00

Dawn Upstairs's two little amateurs arrive. Neither is too fortunate as to her looks, but swoppers can't be choosey and they're quite good enough at twenty pounds a pair. One has a Gorbals accent that could take the point of the walls and a non-nonsense expression round the eyes. I decide to put her on the door. Anyone who can parley his way past her without paying deserves to get in free.

Dawn Upstairs holds an impromptu wardrobe rehearsal and tells them to take their tops off. This they do, whereupon she quickly tells them to put them back on again. Probably right. I wouldn't have dared. Good to have a lady as an associate artistic director. Ladies speak as they find. Mrs. 'arding takes me to one side and explains that she's only here as window dressing, so to speak. That's cool, I say, but better not tell Dawn Upstairs. She's nervous enough as it is.

9.15

Scraggy Janet arrives. Gorbals on the turnstile tries to charge her £20. Good start. Shows she's on the ball, but Scraggy Janet is rather offended. She, Dawn Upstairs and Mrs. 'arding get into a giggly girl's huddle and I have to explain that they can't do this once the customers arrive. Notice for the first time how pilled-up they are and doubt whether they'll remember their instructions once the fun starts. Notice that Scraggy Janet has taken an immediate liking to Mrs. 'arding. Should have foreseen this. Not at all within the overall scheme. Danger of losing two women at once. To be discouraged. Take Janet to one side and remind her that she's here for the fellows. Yes, yes, she says, and she goes back to giggle with Mrs. 'arding. Problem.

9.30

Wandsworth Norman arrives with Plumber and Chauffeur, but no Rita. Stupid little prat. Last minute row, he says. These swoppers! Worse, Plumber and Chauffeur flatly refuse to pay more than a tenner each. Gorbals on the turnstyle, a staunch little thing, won't let them in. Plumber looks a bit useful, so I capitulate. Gorbals looks at me with justified scorn. Send Wandsworth Norman, Plumber and Chauffeur through to the drawing room. Three men and three girls. If the Renwicks and their friends arrive next, that will look rather goow. Only snag is that Dawn Upstairs, Scraggy Janet and Mrs. 'arding are looking at Wandsworth Norman, the Plumber and the Chauffeur as though they're carrying bubonic plague. Scraggy Janet and Mrs. 'arding have got to the hand-holding stage. I take Dawn Upstairs to one side and point out that if the Renwicks are next through the door, she, Scraggy Janet and Mrs. 'arding must appear to be the wives of Wandsworth Norman, the Plumber and the Chauffeur. Dawn Upstairs flatly refuses. Nothing on Earh, she says, could make her pretend to be with any one of them. She is a professional, she says, but there are limits.

9.45

Problem slightly eased by the arrival of Larry the Racing Driver. Nice looking fellow, and he pays his twenty pounds, no trouble. He pairs off happily with Dawn Upstairs and I solve the problem of the spare man by taking Gorbals off the door and pairing her with Wandsworth Norman. She doesn't look too pleased with this arrangement and I may have to give her a bonus at the end of the evening. Suddenly realise that apart from the Renwicks and their friends all our other expected guests are fellows. Take the other little amateur off the bar and make her talk with the Plumber and the Chauffeur. I can work the turnstile and the bar.

9.50

Door bell goes. It's the Renwicks and their friends, thank God.

188

Mrs. Renwick looking lovely in a mink coat. Refuses to check this for reasons that become apparent later. At the time I assume it's because she doesn't trust us. Their friends turn out to be a very cheery Irishman called Jimmy or Jerry and his au pair, a mad Swede, three parts bombed. Feel a bit sleazy taking their money and might not have done had they not pressed it on me. Perhaps I should have left Gorbals on the door. Sixty pounds in my pocket now and the situation is that if the five gonks we are still expecting all turn up we'll have grossed £160 against outgoings (including the drink bill) of £150. That's okay. If the show's an artistic success, the fact that it isn't too profitable won't matter. We'll get the balance right next time. The important thing now is that the Renwicks and their friends think it's a cracker and report accordingly to the Stock Exchange.

10.00

Ricky the Restaurateur arrives and insists on paying by cheque. Bit of a blow. Tell him to make it out to Dawn Upstairs; I hope she'll take it as part of her salary. Should be alright. He advertises his restaurant in *What's On* so he probably doesn't hand round bad gooses too often. Escort him through to the drawing room, where I'm sorry to see the atmosphere is not quite right. In spite of precautions, it's somewhat like a cocktail party. At least everyone is sitting down, but they're talking in a strained fashion about the latest films and the difficulty of parking etc. No signs of fruitiness as yet, except between Scraggy Janet and Mrs. 'arding. Mrs. Renwick looking very poised and Mr. Renwick talking to Gorbals. How do these things get under way? Do I suggest a Paul Jones. Suppose nothing happens? Will I have to give everyone their money back or will the fault be theirs? Go back to my position at the front door. Perhaps they'll get it on behind my back. Slight feelings of panic as at a first night in the old days. Have to suppress a strong desire to leave.

10.15

Bobby in Baby Clothes arrives. Shifty looking little man, but he pays up cheerfully. Can't face going back into drawing room, so send him down the passage on his own. Feelings that we have a turkey becoming more insistent. Don't know which would be worse: more of these horrid little men turning up, which will cause an artistic disaster, or the rest dropping out, which will mean financial catastrophe. Feel that if Ossie in Dry Cleaning and Ruislip Terry arrive now I might tell them that it's all a mistake and send them away. And what about Viscount Swingler? But I've only got £100 so far. Just enough for Scraggy Janet and Dawn Upstairs. I must let in one more punter at least.

10.30

Pluck up the courage to return to the drawing room. Situation could hardly be worse. Scraggy Janet cuddling Mrs. 'arding but otherwise it could be any painful social gathering. Mrs. Renwick sitting on her own, looking elegant and frosty. Why will no one talk to her? Surely she should be right up Ricky the Restaurateur's street? He too is sitting on his own, draped sideways over an armchair, trying to look cool, but in fact only achieving the effect of a punter at a strip show waiting for the fun to start. Dawn Upstairs trying to be vivacious, bless her, and holding Larry the Racing Driver's hand. Mr. Renwick still talking to Gorbals. What about, I wonder. Daren't approach closer to find out. Wandsworth Norman and Bobby in Baby Clothes appear to have hit it off nicely, but that won't get us anywhere. Or perhaps it will. Who can tell? Jerry or Jimmy talking to Dawn Upstairs's other little amateur, but their expressions indicate that both find the conversation fairly heavy going. Jerry or Jimmy's au pair, the mad Swede, is squatting in a corner with pencil and paper, apparently writing her memoirs. This won't make a very lively chapter. I start sending signals to Dawn Upstairs, which after an eternity of eyebrow waggling and jerky movements of the shoulders on my part she correctly interprets as a summons to a conference. We retire to the bedroom.

"How the hell", I ask, "Do we get this going?"

"Don't *panic*", she says, "It's all going very well. The Renwicks are perfectly happy".

She's so stoned that I dont consider her interpretation particularly reliable.

"Do you want me to ginger things up a bit?" she asks.

"Yes", I say.

190

"Okay", she say, "I'll take my clothes off and make a show stopping entrance into the drawing room. That should break the ice".

What a splendid girl. She takes off her clothes and I'm stunned to see what a beautiful figure she's still got. Have to remind myself that that's not the sort of thing I'm here to notice. It's odd though how even at an orgy the sexual instinct can suddenly be aroused.

"Who do I get hold of?" she asks.

Mr. Renwick, I say.

"Okay", she says, "But go and fetch me a drink first. I'll wait here".

I go back into the drawing room as instructed, and bloody hell they're at it! All of them, like rabbits, everywhere! And I'd only been out of the room for three minutes. Maniacs. At it all over the floor like knives! Never seen such an appalling sight in all my life. Dawn Upstairs upstaged good and proper. Don't know where to look. Bodies everywhere. Mr. Renwick, grunting horribly, pinning Gorbals to the floor. Look around for Mrs. Renwick and notice that she alone has been left out. Sitting on her own in a corner, still in mink, still looking frosty. Force myself to go and talk to her. Feel protective towards her, feel I must let her know that we're not all savages here, that there's at least one other person in the room of dignity and sensitivity. Sit down next to her, but can think of nothing to say. Wandsworth Norman plumber approaches, flexing his muscles, and I prepare to protect her honour. Tricky situation. Plumber has paid his entrance fee and the customer's always right. Perhaps I can steer him towards someone else. Dawn Upstairs has just made her entrance and I point fatuously in her direction, like a bad actress in a travel documentary.

"Oh look", I cry, "Over *there*!"

The plumber ignores me and grabs Mrs. Renwick. With a snarl he tears off her mink, revealing her as naked underneath. With a moan of pleasure, she falls backwards to the floor, taking him with her. What a peasant I am. These people actually *like* fucking and being fucked, the *activity* merely, it doesn't matter whom or by whom, anybody will do, it's the *exercise* they like. I retire in terror to my position at the front door. Being clothed in these circumstances is a reverse of the usual nightmare and I'd rather be nicked than lose my tie.

Ossie in Dry Cleaning and Ruislip Terry arrive. Their money brings the take up to £140. I can pay off my obligations.

11.30

Viscount Swingler arrives. A huge, beaming spade. "How's it going, man?" he chortles. He's the largest man I've ever seen. But behind there looms an even larger man. His bodyguard. Unsure of entrance fee for bodyguards, so let them both in for £20. Bodyguard has to come through the door sideways. The Viscount has brought his own sounds.

Retire to the master bedroom to do the books. Income £160. Outgoings also £160 if I give the two little amateurs a bonus of a fiver each. This is okay since I started the evening with £30. Enough to launch the second partouze. Begin to feel we've got away with it. Certainly we have an artistic success, and I'll get the mathematics right next time. Must get more couples. Can't go on paying professionals.

There's a ring on the doorbell, which I ignore since all expected gonks have now arrived. Anyone unexpected must be trouble. Viscount Swingler, however, is not of the same mind. He's been in the loo and now goes to answer the door. Sounds of altercation filter through to master bedroom. Decide I'd better go to investigate. Viscount Swingler is trying to persuade a cross looking little man in a woolly prep school issue dressing gown to part with his money.

"Look man, it's thirty pounds to get in here. How many times do I have to tell you. It's all happening here, man! How about it?"

Cross little man turns out to be our next door neighbour. Usual stuff about some people having to work. I smooth his feathers as best I can and he departs eventually. A bad security leak this, and how about the Viscount adding on a tenner for himself? I send him and his bodyguard through to the drawing room and I retire to the master bedroom for another ponder. At least privacy is easily achieved on these occasions. Swoppers seem to have no desire to sneak off on their own. Realise I could have got a flat with only one bedroom.

Decide to peep once more into the drawing room. An incredible sight. Our guests are locked together like a rugger scrum and, as is the case with a well-drilled pack, a blanket would cover the lot. The Viscount, like a stray loose forward arriving late at a maul, fighting to get into the action. Eventually he decides to climb (the term in Rugby parlance for the habit of trampling over other bodies in an effort to reach the ball) and he launches his twenty stone or so indiscriminately at the pile of bodies. Unfortunately, the first backside with which he comes into decisive contact belongs to Mr. Renwick, who seems at first to enjoy the experience, until he looks over his shoulder to discover the source of these unexpected attentions. Coming face to face with the beaming Viscount, he lets out a squeak of dismay and takes off upwards like a jump jet. Something to tell the chaps on the Stock Exchange, at least. The Viscount tries to get hold of Dawn Upstairs.

"Not me, man", says Dawn and she steers him adroitly towards Mrs. Renwick. Mrs. Renwick disappears beneath the Viscount, groaning with ecstasy. Mr. Renwick looks on approvingly. "Wow, wow, *wow* you aint' *never* been fucked like this Baby", cries the Viscount. Inclined to believe him. Dawn Upstairs working well. Carrying out Scraggy Janet's obligations as well as her own. Scraggy Janet still only has eyes for Mrs. 'arding. Silly of Dawn Upstairs to book her. Hope I don't have to give her a bonus. Retire once more to bedroom.

1.30

Ricky the Restaurateur comes into bedroom to report burglarisation of his trousers. Ridiculous. He says they contained some cash and watch worth thirty pounds. Suspect he's flying a kite as regards the cash and the watch. I point out that they can't have walked away on their own and that he'd better have another look. He wanders off looking cross. There's another ring on the door bell and I go to answer it before Viscount Swingler can charge the police an entrance fee. It's Jerry or Jimmy's mad au pair, mother naked except for her walking shoes. "Been for a stroll", she says. "In the street?" "Yes". God help us, another security leak. And only fifty yards from Chelsea Nick. It's obviously as important to lock these swingers in as undesirables out.

2.00

'arding arrives to collect Sarah. Discovers her under Scraggy Janet. He clips her and they retire arguing. Dawn Upstairs and Scraggy Janet come into the bedroom to say that they consider their job done. Some of the gonks have gone and in their opinion Mrs. Renwick is well qualified to attend to the remainder. I pay them and thank them graciously for their services, and they leave. Splendid girls. Ricky the Restaurateur still moaning about burglarisation of his trousers. I suggest he choose himself another pair. This he does and he then departs.

2.45

Everyone now gone except The Renwicks, Viscount Swingler and his bodyguard. Mrs. Renwick being given a terrible seeing-to by the Viscount and his bodyguard. She won't walk for weeks. Mr. Renwick squatting in a corner talking to himself. Lost his reason, I'd say. Whether from the Viscount's attentions towards himself or his lady wife, it's hard to tell. No one else has reported loss of trousers. Odd. I suppose Ricky the Restaurateur must have taken a pair belonging to the management. That's fair. Too tired to check now. Go to bed and eventually fall asleep to the sound of the Viscount urging himself on to yet more spectacular feats. "You ain't *never* had it this way, Doll . . ."

*   *   *

The Major General's flat may never be the same again. A certain amount of damage was to be expected, but that several ornaments and paintings have disappeared surprises me. Whoever took these might have had the dining room table too, had we not popped it into store. The disappearance of Ricky the Restaurateur's trousers provides another mystery. The odd part is that neither Danvers nor I have suffered a loss in this respect. Ricky definitely departed in someone else's, so somebody must have left without his trousers. A mystery that may never be cleared up.

Danvers, furious at missing the fun, went off at lunch time to ease his disappointment at the Turk's Head. He returned in the afternoon, crying drunk and particularly concerned about his knee-caps.

"My knee caps", he kept wailing, "Oh my God, my knee-caps".

I made him roll up his trousers for an inspection, but I could see nothing wrong.

"They're still there", I said, "as you can see for yourself".

"Yes, yes", he cried pathetically, "but tomorrow they won't be".

I assumed he was having an attack of alcoholic horrors, but gradually he told me a heartbreaking story. About a year ago, it seems, he persuaded an arms dealer called Creek to invest £1,000 in his production of *Shit* in Holland. Unfortunately, Danvers spent this sum on other matters and for the last year he has been trying to cover up this small misappropriation. Creek's accountants have now stumbled upon the truth and since loss of limb is the punishment Creek normally inflicts upon defaulters, Danvers now fears for his knee caps.

In the circumstances his request that I book him into the lunatic asylum in Swiss Cottage that Lord Dynavor recently attended seemed sensible. Expensive, but better than having one's knee caps shot off.

I agreed, helped him to pack and summoned a conveyance. When this arrived I escorted Danvers downstairs and said to the driver "Kindly take this gentleman to the lunatic asylum in Swiss Cottage".

I discovered later that as soon as my back was turned Danvers countermanded my orders and instructed the driver to take him instead to the Star Tavern in Belgrave Square, where he proposed, he said, to have one for the road. He staggered into the Star Tavern, it seems, and collapsed at the feet of Creek himself, who was having a production meeting with some of his performers. Creek, with a true gangster's sentimentality, was mortified to see the state to which his threats had reduced Danvers, burst into tears, dismissed the cab driver, drove Danvers to the lunatic asylum in his own Rolls Royce and agreed to pay for his treatment.

*   *   *

SECOND PARTOUZE. A disappointment after the relative success of the first. Still can't get the couples. To vary the scene slightly, booked a different cabaret through Dawn Upstairs and this time she only charged £80. Stella who Stutters and Daft Danny. Otherwise much the same faces: Jerry or Jimmy with a different mad au pair, Bobby in Baby Clothes, Ricky the Restaurateur (free, on account of burglarisation of trousers), Wandsworth Norman, this time with his wife Rita thank heavens, and two gonks belonging to Dawn Upstairs whose names I never caught. When Jerry or Jimmy arrived I asked him whether we could expect the Renwicks. He said he thought not. Mr. Renwick was last seen sitting in his kitchen with a saucepan over his head still muttering to himself; and Mrs. Renwick apparently has lost her sense of balance, causing her to walk into walls. The partouze didn't have the atmosphere of the first, and we were ten pounds down on the evening. The situation is becoming rather tight.

*　　*　　*

Decide to cancel the midweek partouze and stake everything on Friday's being a triumph. To this end, I asked Dawn Upstairs to book us a couple of crackers: Pretty Marie and French Simone.

"Oooh, I don't know about that", said Dawn Upstairs,' "She thinks she's a film star, does Pretty Marie, and I don't know whether French Simone does parties".

She promised to do her best, however, and she rang back after an hour to say that both had agreed to come after a lot of persuasion, but that the package would cost £150. She said she thought I was mad, but I believe the expense, though painful, is justified. The word must surely have got round a bit by now and enough gonks should turn up on a Friday night to cover the cost. If they don't, I'm done for; but such a possibility is unimaginable. We are, after all, offering a single man the deal of his life, bearing in mind that he now has to pay £30 to visit Big Elaine. Here, for only £20, he can have Pretty Marie or French Simone or both, to say nothing of Wandsworth Norman's Rita, Jimmy or Jerry's latest au pair and even Mrs. Renwick perhaps, if she's recovered her balance. I'm confident they'll be breaking down the door on Friday.

* * *

THIRD PARTOUZE. Pretty Marie and French Simone are the first to arrive. Pretty Marie looking gorgeous. None of my business, but I couldn't help noticing. French Simone a very chic lady and rather intimidating. One would never take this to be her scene at all. Probably isn't. What a pair they make and how right I was to book them! We're definitely going up in the world and I can't wait for the gonks to arrive.

Unfortunately the first, inevitably, is bloody Wandsworth Norman and without Rita. I can't think why I continue to let the little prat in.

Next to arrive is Bobby in Baby Clothes. He's persistent too, but at least he pays. There must be money in Baby Clothes.

Then no one. Odd. After half an hour I become nervous and retire to the bedroom to ring Dawn Upstairs. Don't worry, she says, she's mentioned the occasion to all her punters and she's confident several will be coming. Quite right. It's early yet and I'm worrying unduly. It's funny how often in life's one's worst fears turn out to be entirely justified, but I'm still confident that this will not be such an occasion.

I return to the drawing room. Pretty Marie and French Simone are chatting sweetly on the sofa; Wandsworth Norman and Bobby in Baby Clothes are discussing ways of making money in a corner. By ten-thirty no one else has come. That's ridiculous. On previous occasions the mugs started coming through the door at nine o'clock and most had arrived by this time.

"This is odd", I say to Pretty Marie, trying to sound non-chalant.

"Don't worry", she says.

She's sweet. I calculate that if no one else has come by 10.45 I'll have to send her and French Simone away and give Bobby in Baby Clothes back his £20. That will be humiliating, but not the end of the world. Since the artistes will not have had to perform, I ought to be able to fob them off with their expenses.

Unable to sit out the next nerve wracking fifteen minutes in the drawing room, I decide to ring up 'arding from the bedroom. He might be able to hustle up a last minute punter or two, or even phone the Renwicks. He says he's already spoken to the Renwicks and that Mrs. Renwick is still suffering from loss of equilibrium. He agrees with me that I'll have to send Pretty Marie and French Simone home. If Bobby in Baby Clothes and Wandsworth Norman get their hands on them, they can charge us the full £150 and we'll have had it. What a fiasco.

Sit in the bedroom for a while, pondering the implications and still praying for a miracle. It's 11.15 now and I realise I must face up to the inevitable. No one else is coming and I have the humiliating task of sending Pretty Marie and French Simone away with nothing more than their taxi money. And who's to say that they'll accept that? They've been here for over an hour now and would be justified in cutting up rough. French Simone certainly looks capable of violence.

I drag myself back to the drawing room. Pretty Marie and French Simone not to be seen. Just Wandsworth Norman and Bobby in Baby Clothes still discussing ways of accumulating wealth. Perhaps I've had a bit of luck. Perhaps the prospects of being set upon by either of these two acquisitive dwarfs has caused Pretty Marie and French Simone to cut and run.

"Where are the ladies"? I ask. Wandsworth Norman incidates that they're in the dining room on the other side of the sliding doors. That's very odd, I think, they must be having a conference. I pull back the sliding doors and receive a shock, the impact of which causes me to lurch and drop like a plane hitting an air pocket. Pretty Marie and French Simone, for reasons of their own, are having their own private partouze. Even now I could save the situation. It's not my fault that they've jumped the gun, and the fact that they've retired to a private place indicates that they're following their own inclinations rather than the dictates of their calling. Unfortunately, the sight of Pretty Marie in this context causes me to lose my reason. Scarcely conscious even of the dreadfulness of what I'm doing, I take her by the elbow, propel her down the passage to the master bedroom, push the wardrobe against the door (there's no key and I'm not going to be interrupted by some depraved little swinger) and fall upon her in a frenzy.

98

When this humiliating little episode is over, the full awfulness of what I've done hits me sickeningly like a kick in the knee. I've roasted myself, no less. The management has gone mad, looked the paying customers out, assaulted an artiste and now has £20 to satisfy legitimate claims of £150. Failure to pay actors and actresses is bad enough, but *business girls*!! I'd be lucky not to end up in the Thames. I now notice that Pretty Marie, who had not, I dare say, expected to be assaulted by the management, is looking rather startled. She looks even more startled when I say I can't pay her.

"Oh", she say, and then again "Oh".

I give her the twenty pounds subscribed by Bobby in Baby Clothes and promise to submit the balance of £130 owing to her and French Simone within the next few days. They go away looking bewildered, like girl guides who have had the confusing experience of helping an old biddy across the road, only to be mugged by her once the crossing has been successfully negotiated.

*　　*　　*

I'm out of the party business now and have returned to Emma Jane's flat. The brave little girl has paid off my obligations. Mind you, she's getting a lot of mileage out of my £150 screw, but who can blame her? I've also decided to write my statement out. When Knights and Mason arrive, I'll merely have to sign it. Save everyone a lot of trouble. Living in a brothel isn't everything it's cracked up to be.